HORIZON

WINTER, 1973 · VOLUME XV, NUMBER 1

cHorizon

WINTER, 1973 · VOLUME XV, NUMBER 1

EDITOR IN CHIEF
Joseph J. Thorndike

EDITOR
Charles L. Mee, Jr.
MANAGING EDITOR: Shirley Tomkievicz
ART EDITOR: Jane Wilson
ART DIRECTOR: Kenneth Munowitz
ARTICLES EDITOR: Ormonde de Kay, Jr.
ASSOCIATE EDITOR: Mary Sherman Parsons
CONTRIBUTING EDITORS: Walter Karp, Barbara Klaw
ASSISTANT EDITORS: Kaethe Ellis, Susan G. Ferris
COPY EDITOR: Mary Ann Pfeiffer
ASSISTANT COPY EDITOR: Marya Dalrymple
ASSISTANT TO THE EDITOR: J. Muriel Vrotsos
ROVING EDITOR: Frederic V. Grunfeld

ADVISORY BOARD
Gilbert Highet, *Chairman,* Frederick Burkhardt,
William Harlan Hale, John Walker
EUROPEAN CONSULTING EDITOR: J. H. Plumb, *Christ's College, Cambridge*
CHIEF, EUROPEAN BUREAU, Gertrudis Feliu, *11 rue du Bouloi, Paris 1er*

AMERICAN HERITAGE PUBLISHING COMPANY

PRESIDENT AND PUBLISHER
Paul Gottlieb
EDITORIAL ART DIRECTOR
Murray Belsky
SENIOR EDITORS, HORIZON
Marshall B. Davidson
Oliver Jensen

HORIZON is published every three months by American Heritage Publishing Co., Inc. Editorial and executive offices: 1221 Avenue of the Americas, New York, N.Y. 10020. Treasurer: Marjorie C. Dyer. Secretary: John C. Taylor 3rd. All correspondence about subscriptions should be addressed to: HORIZON Subscription Office, 379 West Center St., Marion, Ohio 43302.

Single copies; $6.00. Subscriptions: $20.00 per year in the U.S. and Canada; elsewhere, $21.00.

Cumulative indexes for Volumes I–V and VI–X are available at $3. HORIZON is also indexed in the *Readers' Guide to Periodical Literature.* The editors welcome contributions but can assume no responsibility for unsolicited material. Title registered U.S. Patent Office. Second-class postage paid at New York, N.Y., and at additional mailing offices.

The Clockwork Society

B. F. Skinner   *Anthony Burgess*

Recently HORIZON asked Anthony Burgess, whose essays have often appeared in these pages, to speak his mind on B. F. Skinner, the famous Harvard behavioral psychologist. The assignment was a journalistic natural. In his now celebrated book, *Beyond Freedom and Dignity,* published in 1971, Dr. Skinner forcefully contended that liberty and free will are mere sentimental and prescientific chimeras. In Skinner's view, all human behavior consists of responses to stimuli. If a certain response to a given stimulus is strongly rewarded, or "reinforced," the individual so "conditioned" will respond in the same way whenever the stimulus is present. No moral choice nor act of volition is involved. Such being the case, argues Skinner, we can use the rigorous conditioning techniques of the scientific psychologist to condition people to behave justly toward all, to love their neighbors, to obey the golden rule and so create a better world than mankind has ever known. To the objection that people would be forced to surrender their freedom, Skinner's reply is that freedom is a fiction. We are already the creatures of conditioning, so we may as well be the virtuous and contented creatures of systematically beneficent conditioning.

To Skinner's rigorous theoretical doctrines, Anthony Burgess took profound exception in an extraordinary and troubling novel called *A Clockwork Orange,* which he published in 1962 and which, coincidentally, was turned into a movie at the same time that Skinner's own book was heading the best-seller list. What made Burgess's novel so remarkable was that he appeared to stack the cards, not against Skinner, but in Skinner's favor.

In the novel, which takes place in a crime-haunted London in the not-too-distant future, the protagonist and narrator is a teen-age hoodlum named Alex. In almost every way he is revoltingly vicious. Beating passers-by to a pulp and raping women are his chief nightly pleasures, which he pursues with great verve as the leader of a moronic gang of teen-age sadists. Burgess does not cheat: his protaganist arouses a genuine sense of repulsion in the reader. Imprisoned for murdering an old woman, Alex is chosen by the authorities as a guinea pig in an experimental program for reducing the crime rate—and here the moral problem arises. A certain Dr. Brodsky, whose views are meant to parallel Dr. Skinner's, has developed a conditioning technique that can turn a thug like Alex into "a little machine capable only of good." The method consists of subjecting him to filmed scenes of violence, torture, sex, and perversion after dosing him with medication that makes him reel with nausea.

After two weeks of this intensive conditioning, any impulse toward violence or lust automatically makes Alex sick to his stomach; only humble, gentle, and self-abasing behavior will drive the waves of nausea away. Here, says Dr. Brodsky, half-contemptuously, is "your true Christian," and in truth Alex's behavior, previously so vicious, is now entirely exemplary. He is, however, a clockwork Christian, a doer of good in spite of himself. Which, then, is the spiritually superior state—to be a vicious thug on one's own or a good man by conditioned reflex? That is the unsettling question Burgess raises in his book, just as it is the question Skinner himself implicitly raises in his own. The two authors' answers are diametrically opposite.

Burgess and Skinner, then, have been dueling for many years, but their weapons are as different as their views. Skinner is an experimental scientist wielding the logic and methods of scientific argument. Burgess is a novelist whose "data" is his own personal experience and whose "conclusions" are the characters he creates and the stories he tells. In a sense, the contrasting weapons of the two antagonists embody their contrasting views. Burgess, the novelist, insists that man knows himself from the inside. Skinner, the scientist, denies the validity of subjective judgments, even about man himself. As the reader can see by turning to page 12, Burgess continues to deploy the strategy of a novelist in his latest encounter with Dr. Skinner. For that reason, it is difficult to judge the outcome of the contest, if indeed any final outcome is possible. The running debate between the truth of logic and the truth of experience remains, as ever, illuminating but endless. W.K.

NATIONAL GALLERY, LONDON

COVER: Typical members of the British squirearchy, Mr. and Mrs. Robert Andrews appear under the lowering sky of their native Suffolk in a detail from an early work by Thomas Gainsborough that is now considered one of the artist's supreme masterpieces. Around 1748, when it was painted, landed gentry such as the Andrews' were able to lead a life of extraordinary privilege and freedom, which is described by J. H. Plumb beginning on page 72.

THE YEAR
973

This illumination from a Byzantine gospel shows medieval laborers pruning and tying vines.

ONE THOUSAND YEARS AGO OUR FOREBEARS

LIVED IN A "DARK AGE."

THEY THEMSELVES DID NOT THINK IT WAS DARK,

AND THEY WERE ONLY HALF WRONG

By MORRIS BISHOP

Some say that a new Dark Age is at hand. They may be right, of course, for history displays a succession of dark ages and bright, and we have enjoyed nearly a millennium of brightness, which is bound to fade some time. If the prophets of despair speak sooth, we might do well to look back to the last Dark Age, which beclouded Europe from the fall of Rome (whenever that was) to the beginning of the brilliant Middle Age in, more or less, the eleventh century. Let us, then, fix our gaze on the state of western Europe in A.D. 973, a convenient thousand years ago. What was our world like? And what were its inhabitants, the forefathers of most of us, like?

Look first to the east, to the Russian steppes. There the Slavs dwelt, and thence they pushed ever westward. They are still pushing. Their flourishing towns, Kiev and Novgorod, rivaled the best in western Europe. The Bulgarians moved into their Bulgaria. The Poles thrust out of Russia to their present home. There, in 966, their duke, Mieszko, was baptized a Roman Catholic, and all his people, by order, were converted overnight. The Hungarians, a people from beyond the Urals, appeared in the West at the end of the ninth century. They ravaged and looted as far as Burgundy; but, defeated by the German Otto the Great in 955, they settled down in their new homeland and became peaceful farmers and devout Roman Catholics. Theirs was the last serious barbarian invasion of Europe, for the rampaging fourteenth-century Turks were hardly barbarians. Henceforth the barbarous foe was to come not from beyond eastern borders but from underneath.

Constantinople was the capital of the Eastern Empire, a centralized state with an efficient standing army, a competent bureaucracy, subsidized schools and hospitals, a sophisticated art and literature fostered by the Orthodox Eastern Church. A Western envoy to Constantinople in 949 was bedazzled by the emperor, richly jeweled, sitting on a golden throne beside a bronze tree with twittering bronze-gilt birds. He was guarded by gigantic lions, lashing their tails and roaring; and at a signal his throne could be elevated on high like a garage greasing-rack.

Islam ruled from India to Spain. It long threatened the whole Western world, but by the tenth century it lost its expansive impetus and settled down to the enjoyment of its culture, to gracious living. In Spain, under the Ommiad dynasty, living could be gracious indeed. The land, scientifically irrigated, bloomed gardenlike, yielding rice, sugar cane, cotton, citrus fruits, as well as wheat and olives. Innumerable workshops produced arms, leather and silk goods, carpets, textiles, and pottery for export as far as China. The capital, Cordoba, boasted a half-million population, seven hundred mosques, many Christian churches and Jewish synagogues, three hundred public baths, a 400,000-volume library, and a university with curriculums in mathematics, astronomy, theology, philosophy, medicine, and law, when there were yet no universities in Latin Christendom.

Arab physicians were famed throughout the West. Poets, and poetesses, too, abounded. Their romantic love songs, with their cult of the inaccessible lady, deeply affected the later Provençal troubadours, and through them our modern conventions of wooing in verse and music, and somewhat in behavior. The Arabs were passionate sportsmen, delighting in archery, polo, horse racing, hunting, hawking, tennis, and croquet. They delighted also in festive parties, with singing girls and abundant wine. (The wine was, of course, prohibited by law, but there was no lack of Christian and Jewish bootleggers.)

We step from Islam into Christendom, and are shocked by the difference. Mostly the Christian West is wild country, repossessed by the dark forest, the home of wolves, bears, wild boars, and in eastern Germany of bisons, or aurochs. It is the home also of outlaws and robbers, and of gnomes and goblins guarding once-sacred trees and springs. Here and there are the marks of abandoned cultivation, hummocks hiding forgotten towns and lost cities, the dwellings of evil pagan ghosts.

The Roman remains, the broken aqueducts and overgrown amphitheatres, seem the work of giants. Old Roman roads march unswerving over hill and dale, but roots and bushes pry their stones apart, and many of the old stone-arched bridges have fallen into the streams. The inhabitants are unconcerned; the broken highways discourage invaders, and honest folk have no need to wander. Over all hangs a sense of ruin, of descent from a greater and happier past. Here reigns the Dark Age, as modern historiographers, in their pride, term it.

Nevertheless, the Western world had passed its nadir, earlier in the century. In 909 a Church synod reported with sober justice: "The towns are depopulated, the monasteries ruined and burned, the good land converted into desert. Just as primitive men lived without rule and without the fear of God, subject only to their own passions, so today everyone does what he pleases, in scorn of human and divine laws and the commandments of the church. The strong oppress the weak; the world is filled with violence toward the defenseless, and men pillage the church's property. Men devour one another like the fishes of the sea."

True enough; but by 973 matters had somewhat improved. The savage Northmen had been bought off by the grant of Normandy as a homeland, and the Vikings, like the Hungarians, came to prefer farming to rapine, Christian doctrine to the service of bloodthirsty gods. The Saracens still piratically roved the Mediterranean; they were established on the French Riviera. From Alpine passes, one of which is still known as Monte Moro, they raided northward, attacking even the Swiss monastery of Saint Gall in

Springtime in the Dark Ages: A pious plowman, heeding the divine injunction to work and to pray, is shown in an eleventh-century illumination driving his yoked oxen and giving thanks to the Lord, who floats by him on a cloud.

954. In the year 972 they took captive and held for enormous ransom the prestigious Abbot of Cluny, Magilo or Maieul, as he was crossing the pass of Great Saint Bernard out of Italy. (Served him right; he was a great destroyer of manuscripts by Virgil and other pagan poets.) This indignity provoked the Count of Provence to wipe out the pirate nests and drive the Saracens back across the sea.

That was all to the good, in the view of those of us who are not of Saracen stock. There were other alleviations in life in the tenth-century world. Few plagues and epidemics are reported. Neglected land was brought back into cultivation, new agricultural techniques improved the yield of thin, exhausted fields. Population increased, with an increase in food production, but usually at a faster rate. Professor Lynn White of U.C.L.A. attributes the population growth and the physical and spiritual betterment of the people to a new profusion of proteins, in the form of broad beans, peas, chick-peas, and lentils. Other scholars perceive a mysterious demographic pulse in the world, for a similar population explosion is evident in China, Islam, and the Scandinavian north.

The Western world of 973 was fragmented, atomized; it was a bundle of localisms. England, to be sure, en-joyed a brief cohesion under Edgar the Pacific (959–975). After pledging allegiance to Edgar at Chester eight lesser kings manned the oars of his boat to row him, as coxswain, down the River Dee. But Edgar died young, and troubles aplenty awaited his successors, including Ethelred the Unready, or the Stupid.

France was a collection of baronies and dukedoms, mutually hostile, united chiefly by opposition to their king. The nominal king of France was Lothair, next to last of the line of Charlemagne; he ruled precariously only over Paris and the Île-de-France, and hardly dared venture beyond the limits of his royal domain.

Italy was a power vacuum. The north was a congeries of nearly independent city-states, imperial fiefs, bishoprics wielding temporal rule. Rome and the surrounding Papal States were the property of the Church. Calabria, Apulia, and the south belonged to the Eastern Empire, Sicily to Islam.

Only in Germany was there a national unity, under Otto I, properly termed the Great. Duke of the Saxons and King of the East Franks, he checked the invading Hungarians, Slavs, and Danes, fostered the Christian faith, and made alliance with Byzantium. In 962 he revived the Roman Empire, with himself as emperor. In our year, 973, his son Otto II became emperor. But his empire was a hollow thing; it had no imperial administration and little control over the mighty dukes, barons, and prelates of Germany. As yet it occurred to no one to call the new Roman Empire holy.

A good share of the fragmented world was precariously ordered by the social-governmental-economic system of feudalism. The word itself, and its vocabulary of vassalage, fiefs, homage, have taken on ugly connotations. To condemn, for instance, our "feudal labor code" is unfair to feudalism. The feudal system arose in response to needs—the need of the poor man for protection and the need of the strong man for soldiers and for upkeep of his strength. Feudalism was a bargain; the poor man exchanged freedom for security, for he would rather be safe than free, and anyway freedom meant little when there was no place to go and nothing to do when one got there.

Feudalism had its elevated doctrine, its ethos of loyalty, courage, honor. The feudal lord was not necessarily an oppressor. His interest was to promote the welfare of his workers, not to starve and destroy them. The system was at least a workable one, based on land and the land's products, not on money. If the serf was bound to the land, the land was bound to him; he could not be dispossessed and driven into an unwelcoming world. Feudalism encouraged a certain peace of mind. Every man's status was fixed, his destiny and his duties clear.

Of course, the feudal ideal was open to dreadful abuse. Force could readily usurp right. A brutal lord could rob, torture, and kill his serfs without offending his overlord or his conscience. He could go to war with his neighbors at will, to adjust a boundary, claim a daughter's or a wife's dowry, avenge a slight to his honor, or merely to beguile boredom. War was the noblest of sports.

Economically, the mark of tenth-century country life was a closed, or natural, economy (or autarky), not a money, or market, economy like our own. Gold and silver coins were seldom seen, but a sheep, a chicken, an egg, had visible value. Life centered in the village, a kind of co-operative for the exploitation of land. The village clustered about the log-built stronghold of the feudal lord, with its flour mill, forge, bakery, and chapel. The village was also a social unit, a club for the organization of country dances, religious celebrations, and (in England) church-ales, in which everyone got drunk in church, for charity. The village bought little from outside —salt, pig iron for the smith, needles, fishhooks, and such. It had nothing much to sell, except farm surplus, and often none of that. Transport was costly and difficult, market fairs rare and widely scattered.

Nevertheless, some villages were growing into market towns, and some centers—such as London, Paris, the Rhineland cities—lingered from the Roman past. These were walled and moated; though the inhabitants crowded together, they prudently left room for gardens, crofts, and food magazines. The present-day Englishman's neat garden descends directly from the medieval croft. The townsmen supported a garrison and an abundance of clerics, for the town became naturally an ad-ministrative center for the Church. Some craftsmen were at work—armorers, weavers, candlemakers, suppliers of church ornaments. And more and more merchants were appearing, to create a new bourgeoisie, men of the bourg, or burgh.

We are ill-informed about trade and commerce in the tenth century. Luxury goods filtered in from the East— silks, muslins, goldsmithery, ivory, spices, but the only purchasers were nobles and churchmen. In return, the West could supply metals, furs, some foods, especially salt fish and English cheese, and French wine, and slaves. The merchants were the bold, the hardy, the clever, mostly ex-serfs, who ventured, and frequently lost, their lives on the perilous roads.

Our Western world was unquestioningly Catholic, although the Church sanctified relics of pagan practice and the simple made of the faith a mere bargain with the saints for preservation and salvation. The papacy set the worst of examples; it underwent a moral slump not to be matched until the coming of the Borgias. Election to the papal throne was controlled by a clique of Roman nobles and the infamous Marozia, mistress of one pope, mother of another, grandmother of a third. Of her grandson John XII Gibbon reports: "his rapes of virgins and widows had deterred the female pilgrims from visiting the tomb of St. Peter, lest, in the devout act, they should be violated by his successor."

In our year 973 Benedict VI was elected; he was strangled, one year later, by direction of Marozia's sister. Papal turpitude did not, however, infect the great structure of the Church. At a council of French bishops in 991 the Bishop of Orleans would dare to characterize the papal regime as the coming of Antichrist.

The bishops were mighty men. As feudal lords, administrators of colossal estates (in Germany as much as a third of the territory), they wielded temporal as well as spiritual power, and they ruled as well as, or better than, their noble peers. At least they were much less likely to go to war.

The spiritual life centered in the monasteries. Some of these, to be sure, settled into a comfortable routine, with a minimum of mortification of the flesh. The monks of Farfa, near Rome, when summoned to reform, rebelled and poisoned their abbot. Even Saint Benedict's own Monte Cassino was relaxed. A certain Calabrian zealot made a pilgrimage thither. Under its walls he heard from within the sound of a guitar; and he was informed that the monks took regular baths. Shuddering, he returned to his hermitage.

Look at two of the monasteries. First, Saint Gall in Switzerland, founded in the seventh century, and the home of a long line of learned and virtuous men. It was self-contained and self-sufficient, with barns and stables, a threshing floor, a grist mill, an orchard. There was a row of workshops for woodworkers, saddlers, cobblers, knife grinders, tanners, woolworkers, bookbinders, goldsmiths, sculptors, and makers of altar ornaments. A hostel served wayfarers, an infirmary with a resident physician cared for the sick.

At Saint Gall learning was prized and encouraged; both sacred and profane texts were beautifully copied. Even Greek was studied and Greek texts produced. Two schools were operated—an inner school for novices and oblates, monks in the making, and an outer school for youths who were to remain in the world. The discipline in the schools was strict, but holidays were celebrated with games, races, shot-putting, and at the end a common bath and wine feast by torchlight. It sounds idyllic—a happy intellectual community, lacking only women and golf.

Saint Gall attracted the earnest, scholarly types, the types that naturally seek out the universities today. They were pious enough, but not given to piety's exaggerations. Cluny was quite different. This was a reform monastery, founded in 910, in protest against the relaxations and abuses within the Benedictine rule. Here the *Opus Dei*, the service of God by prayer and praise, was almost continuous. It was presumed that in recompense for Cluny's unending chants and austerities God might pardon the sinful world.

The community was fed on bread, vegetables, fish, and a little cheese. (And this in the midst of fat, gourmandising Burgundy!) In the scriptorium the monks copied only sacred texts; if they had need to consult a heathen book, they indicated the fact by scratching their ears "as dogs are wont to do, for it is not unjust to liken a heathen to such an animal." The Cluny reform was widespread; eventually it was accepted by 1,450 houses. Clearly it answered a need for deeper piety, for self-sacrifice, for immolation to an ideal. But its inmates are not to be counted among our ancestors—a eugenic misfortune.

The world of 973 had, then, its centers of devotion and of learning, islands in an ocean of ignorance. Most of the identifiable structures of the period were abbeys with their churches. These followed in form the traditions of the Roman, and Carolingian, basilicas, but the choirs were much enlarged to accommodate the singers and clerics, and ambulatories were added to provide for processions and for chapels dedicated to saints, with their relics. Frescoes and mosaics adorned the walls; the good Bishop Adalbéron of Reims invented storytelling windows of colored glass. Stone roof-vaulting was attempted, to replace wood. Particularly in Germany ambitious prelates built imposing structures, as at Augsburg, Magdeburg, Mainz, and Cologne. Their style has been called Ottonian, or Pre-Romanesque, or First Romanesque.

The graphic and minor arts were Church-supported. Sculptors carved birds and beasts on tempting capitals. Craftsmen made jeweled reliquaries, processional crosses, candelabras, chalices; they deftly carved ivory, fired enamels and cloisonné ware, and delicately embroidered vestments. Most notable was the art of bookmaking—calligraphy and illustration. In England the Winchester School developed a representational style, with line drawings of men and women engaged in everyday activities.

In creative literature the period was a barren one indeed, but more artful productions were in formation. The Irish and the Slavs already had their epic poems, composed and sung by minstrels. Latin hymns, rhymed and accented, evidently inspired vernacular imitations; so also did Arabic lyrics migrating into Provence. Simple men, in moments of emotion, made up simple songs about love, or springtime, or tragic death—as they do today, for much greater reward. But no one thought of these popular songs as literature. "The vernacular is good enough for the devil," said an abbot of Saint Gall.

In Latin, only a few love songs and some chronicles and pious exercises remain from our period. But one remarkable achievement demands attention. Hatto I, Archbishop of Mainz, was noteworthily bald. The monk Hucbald of St.-Amand addressed to him a poem of 146 Latin hexameters in praise of baldness. Every word begins with *c* for *calvus*, bald. The opening lines run:

Carmina convitii cerritus, carpere calvos
Conatus, cecinit; celebrentur carmine calvi
Conspicuo clari; carmen cognoscite cuncti.

This may be very freely rendered:

Bighearted baldheads, blasted by backbiting balladeers,
Be briefly besought by bumptious but bantering bard.
Blow, bugles, blow! Be bare-brained baldpates belauded!

A culture that could produce such scholarly whimsy is surely not to be scorned.

At the same time the drama was coming to a fumbling self-consciousness. The Easter liturgy was commonly acted out, with monks and responsive choirs taking the roles of angels and holy women at the Resurrection. And there was the surprising case of Hrotswitha, a nun of Gandersheim, who wrote six Latin comedies in the style of Terence, with saints and miracles for the subject. But Hrotswitha was unique; she had apparently no influence outside her convent.

As for the art of music, medieval men and women were irrepressible singers, for group song is a form of communion. At the feasts of the early Anglo-Saxons the harp passed from hand to hand, and every man sang and played in his turn. King Alfred, in the ninth century, was admitted in the disguise of a minstrel to the Danish camp. In our tenth century Saint Dunstan, at Glastonbury, built a famous organ, keeping jealous Satan at bay with a pair of red-hot pincers. For the first time the bowed fiddle appears. Musical notation was invented, to indicate pitch and duration. The addition of a second voice to unison singing inspired the later development of polyphony.

Science, as we know it, did not exist. The idea of experiment and discovery did not fit with the concept of a fixed creation, ordained from on high. However, agricultural technology improved markedly, and in medicine there were some stirrings of scientific spirit. A researcher has found fifteen medical handbooks dating from the tenth century. In the monasteries a cleric, showing aptitude, was deputed to be leech; he medicined his comrades with herbs and abundant bloodletting, to harmonize the humors and reduce the passions. Surgery was relatively advanced; broken limbs were reset, or, if gangrene appeared, amputated. We are told even of plastic surgery for harelip. Urinalysis was practiced.

A duke of Bavaria tried to befool Abbot Notker Balbulus of Saint Gall

While angels fret and the faithful watch, a soldier of the Lord defeats a platoon of the wicked in an illumination done around 973. It is copied from the Utrecht Psalter, one of the most famous illustrated manuscripts of this era.

by sending him, as his own, the urine of a pregnant woman. Notker announced: "God is about to bring to pass an unheard-of event. Within thirty days the Duke will give birth to a child." Of course, the service of physicians was restricted to the rich and noble. Common folk sought help from wise women and witches who practiced folk medicine. The poor patients were probably no worse off than the rich.

Such, glimpsed in snapshots, was the Western world of a thousand years ago. What were its inhabitants like? How did they think, judge, feel? How did they live from day to day? Can we recognize them as our kin, and ourselves in them?

The mark of their minds was faith, a great comfort. There were as yet few heretics and fewer rationalizing skeptics. The simple man made no distinction between natural and supernatural; the supernatural was natural. A miracle was an everyday occurrence. Reproduction and growth, winter storm and springtime bloom, the body's recovery from illness, seemed miraculous, and very properly, too. Evil spirits had their hellish home only a few yards underfoot; their visits to earth were well attested. The chronicler Raoul Glaber saw the Devil several times,

once by his bedside; he was a little black monster in human shape. Fortunately the angels overhead were just as close, able to watch our acts and read our souls and swoop down to rescue us from deserved disasters. We may have been insignificant little people on this earth, but saints and angels loved us, and we loved them.

Our stay here was brief, our productive years few, for old age came soon. Menaces abounded—famine, polluted water, and tainted meat, infections of ill-tended wounds, and raging diseases, such as malaria, typhoid, diphtheria, dysentery, tetanus, puerperal fever. Infant mortality was high, hence women were expected to be fecund, to marry at puberty and begin their proliferation, a hazardous process. They had to produce perhaps three times as many offspring as today, just to keep the population stable.

Death was a familiar in every household. Perhaps its near presence encouraged a prevailing callousness, or brutality. Monarchs set the example, with their blindings and removals of hands, testicles, ears, noses, and entire heads. Mutilation was a common penalty, for malefactors could seldom pay fines and there were no prisons for their confinement and correction. People regarded suffering as inevitable, indeed

rather amusing, in others. The misadventures of the blind and the halt were a favorite subject for medieval funny stories. Of course, it was understood that a patient sufferer expiated his own sins and those of others.

Nature herself was more cruel than kind. She sent not only dearth and disease but floods and drought and bitter wintry blasts. People simply accepted her afflictions. Maybe they were tougher than we are; but we, too, can be tough if need be, as manifold wartime survivals prove. In the northern winters men hugged the fire, in a drowsy and probably malodorous torpor. (We have few reports of medieval smells; even the delicate gentry did not notice them. Men lived with their animals and bathed only in summer. Clothing was handed down from generation to generation; there was no dry cleaning and only an ineffective soft soap. But a visitor from the Dark Ages would be sickened by the fumes of our civilization.) Darkness, especially in the north, curtailed activity. There was as yet no glass, except in rich churches, and the householder's windows were shuttered against the cold. Indoors, resinous torches or rank-smelling tallow candles cast a feeble gleam, so that women could spin and men whittle spoons, shape farm tools, or weave baskets.

9

Then the story-teller or the ballad singer came into his own.

Food varied with the region and with class. One could map all of Europe with divisions into wine regions, beer regions, cider regions, with a special patch for Moslem Spain, consumer of fruity sherbets (a word of Arabic derivation, by the way). Or one could divide the world into butter lands and olive-oil lands.

The class difference in foods was equally trenchant. The noble ate meat, game, and pastries out of vanity; he was punished for vitamin insufficiency by skin diseases, a furious springtime itch, and occasional scurvy. The peasant had little meat, and that usually only in the autumn, when the less likely pigs and cattle were slaughtered to save winter feed. Their product was certain to be tough; a favorite joke was to refuse the meat and ask for a piece of hide instead. Herrings and other sea fish were plentiful near the coasts. The peasant's staples were vegetables, especially peas, beans, lentils, cabbages, turnips, leeks, and onions, and bread, whether of rye, barley, oats, or wheat. (Children still sing a medieval memory —"Oats, peas, beans, and barley grow . . .")

The important meal came in the evening after the day's work, and the main dish everywhere was a great *pot-au-feu,* the contents being everything available. Honey and fruit in its prime were the only sweetening. Except in bad years, the peasant's food was abundant, though unvarying. We would find it dreadfully monotonous, and complain of the lack of salads, sweets, seasonings, hot drinks. But we have substituted a monotony of our own, with the abolition of seasonal foods. We know hardly a difference between the diets of January and July.

As for housing, our noble ancestors of the tenth century occupied rude wooden strongholds, for the arts of stonecutting and masonry were still little practiced, except in Germany, and building stone and lime and cement for mortar were rarely obtainable. The

noble family, with their retainers, dwelt together in the hall or common room, by night unrolling their straw pallets on the floor. The peasant cottages in which most of our forefathers lived were built of whatever materials lay at hand. In England they were chiefly wattle-and-daub. Upright stakes were "wattled," or intertwined with osiers or twigs, and "daubs," or dabs, of clay and mud were plastered on. A poorly daubed house could nearly dissolve in a downpour.

The roofs were tile or shingle, or thatched straw, an efficient rain-shedder but verminous. A hole in the roof served as a chimney. The floor was of hard-packed mud. This, like our adobe, could be surprisingly durable, but it was likely to freeze and thaw, yield to upthrusting ground-water, and return to its original consistency. Sleeping on wet floors was a potent encouragement to rheumatism. The poorer families crowded into a single room together with their farm animals and poultry, insufficiently housebroken.

The furnishings were scanty — a table, benches or stools, a chest, wooden bowls, mugs and spoons, sometimes a bedstead. Earthenware cooking pots were common. There were no glass mirrors — hence girls were forever staring at quiet pools, to assess their faces and foresee the future. Metals for knives, spades, sickles, axes, shears, nails, skillets, were carefully husbanded. Our peasant ancestors were at least freed from the tyranny of possessions. They owned no more than enough to provide shelter, warmth, clothing, and food, and even that little was sometimes begrudged them. An English abbot told his serfs they owned nothing but their bellies.

Were they happy? The question is perhaps an idle one. The men of 973 did not ask it, or at least they have given us no answer. They did not complain of the absence of comforts and

conveniences they could not conceive of, as we do not miss the amenities to be invented in our future. Their lives were given to labor, but it was mostly labor in common, in the open fields, and except at plowing time and harvest time it was not unduly burdensome. The tempo was slow, the speed-up rare, the assembly line unknown. Tilling the soil among one's mates must be a happier occupation than service to a machine, or to a counter in a bargain basement. A village was small indeed, but it was big enough for social life, for frolics and games and dances, for courtship and exciting rivalries and triumphs. The village was the villager's whole cosmos. He was not aware of anything farther away than the end of a half-day's walk. Beyond lay a world more mysterious than heaven and hell. In his village, his home, he was incurious and probably content.

We are inclined, mistakenly, to equate happiness with comfort. We can buy comfort, not happiness. Not long ago 264 inhabitants of Tristan da Cunha, that very uncomfortable subantarctic island, were evacuated to England under a rain of lava from their volcano. After nearly two wretched years in civilization they begged, and obtained, their return to their happy discomfort.

We need not pity overmuch our forefathers and foremothers of 973. They were fulfilling their destiny, mankind's destiny, preserving the seed of the future, our seed. What if their age looks to be a dark one, in the long roll of ages? In that dark the Western world was stirring, preparing the birth of modern civilization. "If the age was dark," said Lynn White memorably, "its darkness was that of the womb."

In 973 Otto II, opposite, a German feudal king, became ruler of the newly revived Roman Empire, which was yet to be dubbed Holy. He is shown standing on a vaguely Roman-looking chariot handing a document to the abbot of the Saint Sophie Monastery in southern Italy, where the illumination was done nearly a century and a half later.

ottoni Impatoris de omibz rebus cenobio
sce sophie ptinentibus.

A Fable
for Social Scientists

In which our leading practitioner of the trade is quickly and painlessly skinned

BF SKINNER

NOW BEYOND FREEDOM AND DIGNITY

Randolph and I threw ourselves down in the cool, coarse grass just beyond the Emotional Engineering Building.

"Ouch," Randolph cried.

"What is it?"

"There's something—kind of—there. Hit my sacroiliac on the darned—"

It was a stone plaque, evidently intended once for affixation to one of the departmental facades but then neglected; or else wrenched away once from such a facade by joking or rebellious students and hidden, the search to recover it perhaps regarded as not worthwhile by the authorities. Anyway, it depicted an archetypal professorial face with the legend B. F. SKINNER: NOW BEYOND FREEDOM AND DIGNITY.

"Well," said Randolph, "there's a darned thing—"

"Would," I said, "that B. F. be a real pair of initials? In England B. F. means one thing only." I was visiting from Stoke Poges, where I held the Thomas Gray Chair of Elegiac Literature.

"Real all right. All too real. I heard him lecture once, though he didn't really believe there was any value in lecturing. It was his books made him in demand on campuses. *Walden Two* went into a couple hundred paperback impressions."

"Ah, yes." I lighted a celery cigarette. "Utopiography. It came out just after World War Two. The year before Orwell's piece of dystopiography. Rather a curious coincidence. But, of course, that was a time for looking into the future, everybody having made such a mess of the past."

"Nineteen forty-eight," Randolph nodded. "I'll have a watercress one, if you don't mind." We puffed out burnt salad into the summer air. "Funny thing, neither of those two books looked into the future. Orwell intended to call his book *Nineteen Forty-Eight*. The great thing about the little Skinnerian utopia was that it was happening here and now—there and then really, of course. Those things were possible *now*, meaning then."

"A lot of it comes back to me," I said. "They were curiously similar, those two books. They were both about controlling the individual, subordinating him to the community. Reinforcement technique—charming old-fashioned term. Negative for Airstrip One, contrive conformity through fear of pain; positive for Walden Two, induce conformity through hope of pleasure. Something like that."

"Free will," Randolph mused. "Old Skinner gave that one hell of a kick in the fanny. If men are free, they're not capable of behavioral conditioning. But they *are* capable, et cetera, et cetera, therefore they're not free."

"Semantic tyranny," I said. "*Freedom* is as emotionally loaded as *mother*. He was right, of course. That title of the other book—the one there: *Beyond Freedom and Dignity*—that was meant to shock. The very blasphemous notion of getting *beyond* those ultimately desirables. And yet what do they really mean? Hangovers from old sermons, ancient political diatribes, forgotten war chants. Like *sin,* they are words that have no real meaning."

"You tell my old man that and see what he'd say," Randolph replied.

"Oh, but seriously—"

"Okay, okay, let's leave theology out of it. Funny, my old man says that, too. I'm echoing my old man. What he says about theology is that it's a higher game. He sticks firm to two propositions—good and evil."

What does he mean by evil?"

"He won't define it. He says you can recognize it almost by smelling. It's as real, he reckons, as the scent of catnip to a cat. When I used to say that the good-evil opposition was only the same as the right-wrong one, he used to tremble with rage. Still would, but I try not to rile him any more."

"Well, it *is* the same, isn't it? Right and wrong are relative things, variable, set up according to the community's needs. It was hygienically wrong for the old Semites to eat pork—because of tapeworms, I suppose. Then it be-

comes an infraction of Jehovah's law, or Allah's, just to stress the danger. It ends up as evil."

"His point used to be that evil was a great permanency, while wrong was something that, as you said, changed according to expediency."

"Did he give examples of evil?"

"Well, yes. Killing, of course."

"But that's not always evil, any more than it's always wrong. I mean, you kill the armed intruder, if you're able. The community orders you to kill the enemy who tomorrow may be your friend."

"Well, there you hit on his point. You could do right, but at the same time the right could be evil. I mean, you kill the enemy—the Japanese this year, the Vietcong the next—and you rightly become a hero, but you've also committed evil. See his point? If we're carnivores—and he's still a big steak man, I can tell you—we'd better eat meat, but at the same time we're committing evil by taking life. He said we can't really stop committing evil, we're sort of committed to it in order to stay alive, but we ought to recognize it for what it is. Original sin he sometimes called it."

"Another nice old-fashioned term. It seems to me that evil, in your father's deliciously simple canon, is just another word for killing. Have another cigarette."

"Parsley and thyme, if you have one. Good. Thanks. This is killing, too, in a way. Not ourselves, of course, not any more, but the living plant we dry and consume. My dad's idea is that every single thing that can be thought of as possessing organic life—a painting, a poem, a cat, a spirochete—has a basic right. This right is to be itself, be everything it was genetically willed to be, if one can use that phrase, and everything it chooses to be out of its own will. To interfere with this right is evil. So if you torture an animal, wantonly, or even in the service of science (which may, of course, be *right*), then you interfere with what it wants to be, what its pattern proclaims, so to speak, and this is evil. Ah, we have company."

The company consisted of Wanda and Chuck, nice and very wholesome sophomores whose surnames I found it impossible to remember. "Hi," they said, and we said, "Hi." They lay down and began chewing grass, Wanda exhibiting a fine tract of egg-smooth leg as far as the thigh. "Who's that?" Chuck said, frowning at the disingraminized plaque. "Oh, Skinner. We did *Walden Two* in high school. Kind of a utopian idea," he defined for our benefit.

"We were talking about free will and ethical choices. Evil and so on," I said. "Do you kids feel free to choose between good and evil?"

"I was brought up Calvinist," Wanda said. "Everything is worked out for you before you are born. Damned or saved, and you can't do a thing about it. Of course, it's logical—"

"Logical, my foot," Chuck said.

"—Logical in the sense that if you have an omniscient God, then he knows what you're going to do, down to how many times you go to the john in your lifetime. If he knows you're going to go—oh, say, seventy thousand times—"

"That's a lot," Chuck said.

"Well, it's just an example. Seventy thousand times, then you're not free to go sixty-nine thousand nine hundred and ninety-nine times."

"Sounds like Walden Two," Randolph said. "You've got Skinner here controlling everything, like a Calvinist God, so that you seem to be free, and he knows you're not—the big behavioral engineer grinning down from the clouds. He knows, but you don't."

"The rule of experts," I said. "The rule of those who know best. I don't go for that."

"You've gone for it all right," Randolph said. "We've all gone for it. We used to smoke tobacco, now we smoke dried vegetables. The U.S. government began with the banning of cigarette commercials, then it ended up with the banning of cigarettes and fi-

nally, to be on the safe side, all tobacco products. This was to save man from himself. Man must change himself if he's going to survive. That's Skinner's main thesis."

"I leave it to you," I said, grinning, "to amend that to: men must change other men. The knowledgeable must change the ignorant. The ignorant will resist. With the *good* knowledgeable the changes will be made through positive reinforcements."

"What do you mean by the *good* knowledgeable?" Wanda asked.

"Those who seek nothing for themselves. Those who love man and don't want him to kill himself. The Planners and Managers of Walden Two, who really have quite a rotten time. Not many positive reinforcers for them, none of the panoply of power or admiration. Christs in a way."

"But do these Christs exist?" Wanda inquired.

"There was Skinner himself."

"A point that Skinner makes," I remembered, "is that this notion of being engineered by the pure-minded behavioral technologues may not be to everybody's taste now, in the present, but that we've no right to legislate for the future. There'll have to be a new kind of human being, one who'll see nothing wrong in having his aggressions trimmed. The question is: when do we start? When does the present become the future? Do we let the technologues take over a batch of month-old kids and start work on them in a fine rational hygienic complex in the woods—one built perhaps with Skinnerian royalties?"

"Not my kids," Wanda said. "I can bring up my own kids, thanks very much."

"You're one of the good enlightened disinterested knowledgeable," Chuck said, smiling. "Pity your subject isn't behavioral technology."

"This is the trouble," sighed Randolph. "We all think we know best for our kids, but, of course, as Skinner's Waldenians point out, we don't. We're not going to get that utopia. Look, we

must get back to this main point. About freedom, I mean. To hell with dignity."

"Right," Chuck said.

"Freedom only really matters in this area of choosing between good and evil, and that comes down, I suppose, to choosing not to do evil. There can't be any harm in teaching people to recognize evil, can there? I don't mean through persuasion, but through demonstration."

"Demonstration?" Wanda didn't like the sound of that.

"Yes. From books, films, newspaper reports, and so on. Now then—a very awkward question: what do we do with people who, in full awareness, commit evil?"

"I'm afraid there's nothing *positive* we can do." The lengthening shadow seemed to etch a new, sardonic look on the Skinner plaque. "All we can do is preach and teach, but without much hope."

"That's pure Judaeo-Christianity," I said. "And there'll have to be accessories of anger and threat and punishment."

"Threats of eternal punishment," Chuck said. "At least those do no real harm. They don't corrupt the threatener."

"So we're back where we started," I said. "Skinner at least had a positive and optimistic program. Beyond freedom and dignity means beyond evil." I deliberately didn't complete the symmetry with a mention of *good*. It was something we hadn't defined and probably never would define. "No evil in Walden Two," I added. "Back to Eden, complete with plumbing and stereophonic music."

"So," Randolph said bitterly, "we have to manufacture a new kind of human being."

"Let's submit," I said. "And then somebody can write a book about an alternative society. I could do it myself. You enter your imaginary city through a dim-lit stone gate thronged with poxed beggars and mangy dogs. You enter, you walk on cobbles under flickering lamps, slithering on effluent poured from upper windows. Children whimper or howl, having been beaten into obedience. Loud song comes from the taverns, a bearded, balding man is to be seen by candlelight writing a five-act tragedy. Prostitutes abound. Food is cooked on spits over wood fires. Barrels spill wine, tobacco fumes make pestilent the air. From an ornate baroque church polyphony pours out, some anthem about man's redemption. Christmas is coming, and the cribs are decorated with rags and holly. An evil monarch rules, spies and torturers are everywhere —"

"It sounds like downtown New York," Chuck said.

"It sounds all right," mused Randolph. "Let's leave perfect societies to these new Skinnerian men. The only question is: when does it start? I've nothing against Walden Two, for other guys. I just don't want it myself. That ought to mean nobody wants it."

"Dinnertime," Wanda said.

We went in together, leaving Skinner's simulacrum to have its now enigmatic features obliterated by the coming summer night. In the cafeteria we helped ourselves to tea in long glasses, carrying them to our tables in plaited straw holders. That, I remembered, was an idea taken from *Walden Two* — nonspill tea-bearers. It's always the inessential things that get through.

"Walden One," Randolph said, as he drank his soup. "It worked for him, but it was inhuman. Eden before Eve. All we can do is to push back the frontier a little, painfully. The pain is conceivably important. Without pain there's no art, for instance. Can you imagine the novels and poems and plays that come out of Walden Two? No conflict to be resolved, no agony to be cathartized."

"Well," said Chuck, ketchupping his hamburger, "I'd rather do without *King Lear* than put up with the human agony it sprang out of. I'd rather not have the *Eroica* than have the big bloody conqueror it tries to immortalize."

"Calligraphic art," I munched, forking in beans. "That's all you'd have in your bloody utopia — sorry, I ought to say bloodless. Or, if you wanted great films and fiction and poetry, you'd have to feed off the non-utopian world. Walden Two is parasitic in that respect. Symphony orchestras are being painfully supported in the big world outside, and Walden Two activates the ears of its tape recorders. But to get your point straightened out, Chuck. You say you'd gladly do without, say, great tragic art if you could eliminate its subject matter from the world. The fact is that, as Skinner indicates, you can clear out that subject matter. Now then, what are you going to do in your spare time — when you've done your four-hour stint or whatever it is?"

"I don't follow you."

"You'll eat, make love presumably, walk, play tennis or chess, and sleep. How about your emotional life?"

Love. There's a great thing about the American habit of eating with one hand only: a lover can always grasp the loved one's hand, the disengaged one, I mean.

"You mean emotional tempests, jealousy, kissing and making up?"

"If I read Skinner right, there'll be no jealousy. *War and Peace* won't make any sense. There'll be no burying your head in a good book."

"Or in the morning paper," Wanda said, smiling. "No news, except the results of the chess tournament. Rather restful, I should think."

"It's so *totally* a new man that's needed," cried Randolph. "So new that he'll be a Martian. Walden Two's strictly for Martians."

"What it boils down to," I said, eating Boston cream pie, "is that that sort of community has to be a pocket in an imperfect society, the escape hatch. It will have to exist by virtue of the imperfect society, defined by it. We have these communes already — kids living together in peace and amity and a complete ignorance of agronomy and animal husbandry. It's like drug-taking or what used to be called hippydom: you take it as a bizarre and perhaps salutary slash of color across society, but it can never be society itself."

"It can, it can," cried Randolph. "That's the whole idea. And it will be good for those who are conditioned to it. But the point is: *it has to start.* And it can only start in a takeover of freedom. After the takeover everything will be fine. But we have to resist the takeover. *We have to:* we'll be untrue to ourselves if we don't. Therefore the takeover can't succeed, for it won't have sufficient enforcement power. So there'll be no Wal —" His jaw suddenly dropped, disclosing the remains of an unchewed mouthful.

"What's the matter?" I said.

"This is it, this is all he was describing —"

"What?"

"All he was describing was one of the better state universities. Shorn of lectures, essays, and examinations. A man can't get away from his background. Have you ever," he asked me, "been to London?"

"Of course," I smiled. "I was born there."

"Sorry, I was forgetting. George Orwell made his Ministry of Truth out of the BBC's Broadcasting House, and the torture chamber, Room 101, was named for the studio in the cellar where he did his broadcasts to India. In the same way, old Skinner made his Walden Two out of the university world he knew. And all that business about a technology of behavior — it's just classroom talk. Thank God, we don't have to worry. Skinner didn't mean it after all. We're free."

Free as the moonbeams that now silvered the stone face in the grass, through which stoats would hunt and kill and a silent insect drama go on. Skinner, skinned newly by the moon.

"You said," said Randolph, "that in England B. F. meant only one thing. I used to know, but I've forgotten. Tell me."

I told him.*

*Bemused Fictionalizer.

The old order crumbles in a university town: with a photomural of Berkeley, California, as a backdrop, three radical members

The Berkeley Clock

The model city of American liberalism
is currently under siege.
Will it go down? If it does, where does
that leave the rest of us?

A crisis of liberal civic culture occurs when its best substantive virtues—equality, liberty, fraternity —become so enlarged and amplified as to shake its procedural framework.

—Professor Paul Seabury (Berkeley)

For the past ten or twelve years, I have been keeping an eye on Berkeley, sometimes from the streets of the city itself, but more often from the deck of my house on the opposite shore of San Francisco Bay. On a clear day, with the help of binoculars, I can read the time on the great clock on the campanile at the heart of the campus, but the air has been growing thicker and heavier around here, and it is not often nowadays that I can tell the hour from the Berkeley clock.

of the city council refuse to pledge allegiance to the American flag at the first council meeting after their election in April, 1971.

The progressive obscuring of Berkeley is unhappily not merely a matter of the chemistry of hydrocarbons in the air. Nor is it directly a result of the student upheavals that since 1964 have made Berkeley a familiar name in Bulgaria, Peru, and Madagascar—although, God knows, there is still more than enough activity in this department. A friend, a man of humane and liberal instincts, who happened to be in downtown Berkeley last May told me later, in tones of controlled outrage: "What can only be described as a mob of hundreds of people marched through the Shattuck Avenue business district. The rocks and bricks began coming through the windows of the place where

I was, and we were herded into the basement and cowered there while that place was turned into a shambles, as was the entire main street. I cannot think that slowed the bombing in Vietnam."

As I write, the streets of downtown Berkeley still look as if street fighters had worked their way from building to building, but this air of battle is only the outward appearance. Berkeley's real trouble goes much deeper, but claims few headlines outside the city limits. During the past two years, i.e., since the winter of 1971, a great rent has been torn in the civic fabric, and there are those among the population who will tell you that the city has suffered a

mortal wound from which it may never fully recover.

The future of Berkeley is a matter that should concern us all, because for many years Berkeley has been a world capital for the liberal state of mind. By any calculus of civic imagination and progressive-mindeness, Berkeley has for a hundred years been a special place, a paradigm of the intentional community, with the university as its heart. Of Berkeley's present population of about 120,000, 27,500 are students at the university, while 15,000 more are alumni of the university. For its citizens—both those who are connected with the university and those who are not—it has presented a civi-

By KENNETH LAMOTT

Shouting, gesturing, and interrupting, Berkeley student activists pack the gallery at a city council meeting, cockpit for stormy battles between radicals and the town's once-dominant liberals.

lized alternative to big-city life that does not condemn its inhabitants to the insipidities of the suburbs.

In counting Berkeley's civic virtues, let us consider the following items:

¶The population of Berkeley represents a higher concentration of college-educated citizens than can be found in any other community in the country.

¶Berkeley began to desegregate its public schools in 1964, and by 1968 it had become the first school district in the country to desegregate completely through busing.

¶In 1923 Berkeley was one of the first cities (after Dayton, Ohio) to adopt the city-manager form of government. Its municipal government has been widely praised for its competence, honesty, and efficiency.

¶Since 1906, when August Vollmer reorganized it, the Berkeley police department has been an example for police throughout the world. It was Vollmer (himself self-educated) who proposed the model of the policeman as a college-educated professional. Recruits to the police force are still required to have two years of college.

¶The consumer co-operative movement has been a highly visible and important part of Berkeley's economic life for almost forty years. Since its founding in the mid-1930's, the Berkeley Co-op has become the largest in the country, with sixty-five thousand member families, about a third of whom live within the city limits.

Let me also add my observation that the *personality* of Berkeley contains an attractive quality that I have not detected in the other university towns I know. New Haven and Cambridge are, once one leaves the campuses, rather grubby industrial towns. Boulder and Madison are pleasant enough but uninteresting. Palo Alto is both uninteresting and Higher Suburbia. Only in Berkeley have I had the feeling that town and gown are all of one piece in a truly liberal community.

This prevailing liberalism may contribute substantially to the sense of impending doom that one can detect among many people in Berkeley. As Paul Seabury, who teaches political science at the university, wrote of the current atmosphere (in a dour article in *Commentary*), "It is as though the harpstrings of the liberal conscience were electronically hooked to a giant amplification system; and all plucked simultaneously."

I have this lovely home my husband and I built in 1920 and now none of my friends will come to visit. —*A Berkeley Woman*

The land on which Berkeley stands forms a great amphitheatre on the eastern shore of San Francisco Bay. In its natural state a land of hills and oaks, it was originally part of the domain of the Costanoan Indians. Then came the Spaniards. A sergeant named Luís Maria Peralta received the land that was to become Berkeley as part of the great Rancho San Antonio, granted him for his faithful service. Peralta divided his lands among his four sons, of whom Domingo received Berkeley. In 1849 the Americans came, bringing their twin hungers, for gold and for land; in 1853 Domingo Peralta had to sell all his inheritance except for a three-hundred-acre homestead.

From its beginning, Berkeley was planned as a college town. When, in 1866, the trustees of the (then private) College of California were planning to build their campus among the oaks, one of them, Henry Durant, quoted George Berkeley's line, "Westward the course of empire takes its way." A colleague of Durant's suggested they name the town after the bishop, and so Berkeley got its name. The College Homestead Association was formed to subdivide the land, and the sale of lots was encouraged by inviting would-be buyers to take part in picnics on the bucolic site. The names the developers gave to the streets around the campus bear witness to Berkeley's built-in high-mindedness: Addison, Allston, Bancroft, Channing, Dwight . . .

Incorporated in 1878, Berkeley's growth was hastened by the great San Francisco earthquake and fire of 1906, which brought an infusion of dispossessed San Franciscans to its hills. The town shook itself down into its present socioeconomic geography: the Hills, the Campus, and the Flatlands. For a couple of miles parallel to the bayshore, where the main line of the Southern Pacific bisects the Flatlands, there is some light industry. The rest of the Flatlands is occupied mainly by decent single-family bungalows, originally the homes of factory workers but now the homes of most of Berkeley's black citizens, who make up about a quarter of the population. There are no recognizable slums. The Campus area includes the campus proper and the surrounding business districts and civic center. The Hills are where the prosperous folk, both white and black, live. (This is, of course, something of an oversimplification, but it will do for our purpose.)

During the years in which the town and university grew and prospered, the word "idyllic" was not infrequently used to describe the "city of homes." It was, by all accounts, an extraordinarily pleasant and innocent town as well as a liberal one. An observer in the 1930's commented on the "gay bustle of the streets surrounding the campus— streets thronged with men students in corduroys and gaudy sweaters, women students in mock peasant head kerchiefs and jaunty little half socks."

And, of course, Berkeley remained firm in the liberal, humane, progressive faith. In the dark days of 1942, when even Earl Warren and Walter Lippmann were rendered paranoid by the presumed latent treacherousness of the Japanese-Americans, the women of Berkeley were sadly giving farewell parties and packing box lunches for their Nisei and Japanese friends, bound under the infamous Executive Order 9066 for bleak camps in the western desert.

The gaiety, the liberalism, and the Bohemianism survived for almost twenty years after World War II. A young woman I know who dropped out of Mills College in the mid-1950's to live in Berkeley with her boy friend and go to the university, recalls that "there's always been a Bohemian life. I mean, I lived on Panoramic Way, which has a gorgeous view of the entire Bay Area, and has both very expensive professors' houses and run-down shingles. I had a place for fifty-five dollars a month and a million-dollar view. It was known as Heartbreak Hill. Everybody on that street was either shacking up or was homosexual. We wore sandals to class and our hair long."

Then came 1964 and the Free Speech

Polarization: Mayor Warren Widener, left, who had the radicals' support, presides over a stalemated meeting as Councilman Borden Price, a moderate Republican, looks on in quiet vexation.

Movement and all its sequelae, and nobody ever again thought to comment on the "jaunty little half socks" of the girls on campus. Rather, the hallmark of the Berkeley girl became her unfettered bosom, jaunty in its own way perhaps, but implying promiscuity and worse to solid citizens of the sort who put Ronald Reagan into office.

The last time I recall seeing public gaiety in Berkeley was Memorial Day, 1969, a date precisely fixed in my memory because it was the occasion of a great triumphal march celebrating the student victory—or what seemed to be a victory—in the matter of the People's Park. I had gone to Berkeley to report on the event, but soon found myself carried away as part of the euphoric crowd, a daffodil in my hand.

When I commented on this phenomenon in the course of a recent conversation with the police chief, Bruce R. Baker (who is himself a Berkeley graduate), his long, angular face lit up as he said, "That was a catharsis. Everybody was happy—you surely observed the policemen that day. It was just that the boil had come to a head and burst." Then he added somberly, "A month or two later, that feeling was dead."

The civic troubles with which Berkeley is now struggling can trace their lineal descent to the student troubles of

the 1960's, but they have a character all their own. It is a situation of massive ironies, in which the city has become polarized between, not liberals and conservatives, but liberals and radicals, and in which the institutions being shaken in the cold wind are precisely those in which Berkeley has historically taken great pride: the professionalized city government, the first-rate public schools, the civilized police, and even the Berkeley Co-op.

Here are some fragments from a lunchtime conversation with Sheila Johnson, the dropout from Mills who eventually took her doctorate in anthropology. She is an attractive, freshfaced woman of thirty-five.

"For three years just after my husband had finished his degree we didn't have a car, and our only recreation was to walk to the campus during the day or to walk in the evening down the darkened streets to catch a movie or to sit in a coffeehouse or to visit Fred Cody's and rummage in books until midnight and then have a cup of *cappuccino*. This was our life, and all that has changed. You can't do that any more. Cody decided about three years ago to close at five o'clock because the only people who came into his place at night were drug addicts who ripped him off and sold his books for money for drugs. . . ."

"Many of the things that made Berkeley so pleasant are being eviscerated by this whole thing. . . .

"The Berkeley scene is very troubling, partly, of course, because it has an enormous student-body population which can vote and can be organized. . . .

"The city council has been in utter chaos ever since the April [1971] elections. Meetings run until three in the morning over such issues as Berkeley's signing a separate peace agreement with Hanoi, that sort of thing. . . .

"My husband calls the radical councilmen Tonton Macoutes. They are really hard-core revolutionaries designed to be so obstructionist that the system will come to a halt."

We are confronted with a continual series of one-shot high-profile radicalizing issues, but we can't formulate meaningful plans.

—Councilman Edward E. Kallgren

And so—at last!—we have arrived at the eye of the hurricane, the center of this civic maelstrom. During the past two years the center of gravity has shifted from Telegraph Avenue six blocks west to the architecturally undistinguished city hall. On the second floor is the city council chamber, a large room decorated with a photomural of the city and furnished with wood-slatted folding chairs. The council-people sit on a raised dais, each identified by a nameplate: Ms. Hone, Mr. Kallgren, and Mayor Widener are generally identified as liberals; Mr. Sweeney is a middle-of-the-road Democrat; Mr. McLaren and Mr. Price are Republicans, conservative and moderate respectively; Ms. Hancock, Mr. Bailey, and Mr. Simmons call themselves radicals. Messrs. Sweeney, Widener, Bailey, and Simmons are black.

The council sessions I have attended have been quiet, and for that reason quite untypical. (The agenda of one of these, however, was all too familiar to Berkeleyans—a five-page document of sixty-five items, including matters such as funding for the Soul Site Kick Pad.) When I asked Edward E. Kallgren recently how things had gone at a meet-

A bulletin board at People's Park mirrors the interests and causes of the young; it includes instruction in how to "recycle" garbage into compost. Concern for the environment is an almost universal passion among Berkeleyans, whether or not they are able to agree on any other issue.

ing the previous night, he said, "Bailey called me a buffoon, and I said I didn't have to stand for that, and got up and walked out. That ended the meeting since they didn't have a quorum."

In a microcosmic way this is what has been happening since the present council took its seats—a standoff between radicals and liberals, name-calling, the postponement of pressing action, and a pervasive sense of frustration and paranoia. A downtown businessman, Paul Harberts, who owns a sporting goods store, told an appre-

ciative audience not long ago: "The mayor of the city incites the masses in Sproul Plaza; the city council declares a Day of Mourning for the enemy; reparations for the enemy are advocated and narrowly defeated by the council; the American flag is burned in the streets; the ensign of the enemy is flaunted on Shattuck Avenue; council sessions are circuses. The ultimate responsibility for this insanity lies in the citizenry of this once idyllic city." The speaker went on to charge that the civil service was being "dismantled before our very eyes" in order to make room for blacks and other minority employees. *Mutatis mutandis*, Mr. Harberts's complaints surely awakened sympathetic echoes, even among Berkeleyans who consider themselves casehardened liberals.

The creation of this Frankenstein's monster—for surely this is what the city council is in relation to the traditional liberals—came about during the 1971 elections, in which five seats were being contested. When three radicals were elected, there was editorial rejoicing from as far away as New York City, where the *Times* welcomed the election of radicals into the establishment. The question many Berkeleyans are considering now is whether the establishment can survive the experience in any useful form at all.

Ilona (Loni) Hancock (thirty-one), D'Army Bailey (thirty), and Ira T. Simmons (twenty-nine) were carried into office by a coalition formed of the Black Caucus and an organization called the April Coalition, which was largely white and drew most of its strength from the student vote. (Among the other groups represented in the April Coalition were Men's Liberation, Gay Women's Workshop, the New Democratic Coalition, and Ecology Action.) Ronald V. Dellums, the representative from California's Seventh Congressional District, was (as described in *Ebony*) the "big daddy of the coalition and its titular head." Tom Hayden, who was then living in Berkeley, played a part in the campaign, along with the Red Family Commune.

In retrospect, the serious campaign issues, as opposed to those that were largely revolutionary rhetoric, were concerned with the city administration—the radicals attacked the city-manager system head-on, advocating its replacement by a network of neighborhood councils that would carry government to the people—and with the police. For all their relative sophistication, the Berkeley police have not always made things easy for themselves. On July 4, 1970, Mayor Widener, then a councilman, was asked to intervene with the police after a Berkeley minister had been beaten into unconsciousness by police. Widener, who is young, handsome, and black, went to police headquarters to lodge a protest. He was thrown out on his ear. Widener complained to the city manager. He was thereupon invited to return to headquarters, where he was ceremoniously received by a police captain.

The campaign against the police was framed in a measure that would abolish the existing police force, replacing it with three separate and autonomous forces, one for the Hills, one for the Campus, and one for the Flatlands. The "police amendment," also voted on, went down by more than two to one. The three radicals, however, were elected, and Councilman Warren Widener, who was thought to be sympathetic to them, was elected mayor. Besides the organized students, the radical constituency included the black vote (even though most of Berkeley's black citizens are essentially conservative) and the Hill liberals, who presumably voted for the radicals on the general antiestablishmentarian principles that we liberals hold dear.

A readjustment of the expected alliances became apparent at the council's first meeting, when Mayor Widener declined to join the radicals in refraining from the salute to the flag. The issue was solved by deleting the patriotic exercise from the agenda of succeeding meetings. (The councilmen of the neighboring town of Albany thereupon began saluting the flag twice, once for themselves and one for their fallen brethren.) The mayor further alienated himself from the radicals by appointing a liberal (Ms. Hone) to a vacant seat, thus breaking the possibility of a radical stalemate-veto whenever they could convert one of the liberals to their cause.

The lack of a majority has not rendered the radicals impotent, although to an outside observer like myself it seems that little has actually been done

—there has been no dramatic transfer of power to the people, no red flag hoisted above city hall, no ceremonial evacuation of the offices at the police department. In spite of what John R. Coyne has suggested in the *National Review*, Berkeley has not yet become the first "honest-to-God New Left Democratic People's Republic on the continental United States."

Actual accomplishments have included a year-long partial freeze on hiring in the city civil service while an apparently interminable argument went on about an affirmative-action policy—the accelerated hiring of minority people. The police department has particularly been under attack and has suffered from a steady attrition in its ranks. Ms. Hancock, a pretty and very bright young woman, has described the radicals' achievements in terms of having brought about the resignations of opponents in the city administration, increasing the power of the neighborhood associations, and shifting the "community dialogue" to the left.

Virtually the only comfort the majority on the council has had has come from observing internecine bickering among the radicals. When there has been a discussion of city hiring policies, as there often has been, Ms. Hancock has called the black councilmen sexist, while Messrs. Bailey and Simmons have retorted that their colleague is no better than a racist. Tempers get sharp, and voices grow bitter, and the viability of the radical coalition itself has publicly been called into question.

What has happened in Berkeley that is truly destructive is that the classic liberal-conservative accommodation, made possible by some shared notions about acceptable political strategies, has been replaced by a rapidly polarizing situation in which little chance for accommodation is offered. As Councilman Kallgren described his perceptions to me, the goals of the liberals and radicals differ less than their willingness to come to terms with each other. "The essential difference from a practical point of view," said Mr. Kallgren, who is a dark-haired, owlish lawyer, "is the unwillingness of the radicals to make certain kinds of compromises, to come to deal with and treat with the more liberal councilmen. I think they do this for ideological reasons. I think they *want* to see the situation polarized. They would prefer to talk endlessly or to raise issues time after time in order to keep the situation alive and burning rather than make a reasonable kind of compromise."

The sense that something serious is going wrong in the city has not been eased by the air of a fundamental mystery that still surrounds the two radical black councilmen. D'Army Bailey, a tough and aggressive graduate of Yale Law School, arrived in Berkeley just in time to register for the 1971 elections. He and his colleague, Ira T. Simmons, also a nonpracticing lawyer, apparently live in considerable comfort on the $300 a month they each receive as councilmen and maintain a staff that has been estimated to cost somebody $3,000 a month. Their answers to money questions have been vague, and even Congressman Dellums has suggested that more candor in these matters would not be a bad thing.

It is not hard to understand why Berkeley, this most civilized of cities, should have fallen victim to a sense of despair, paranoia, and a serious erosion of civic morale. Even the Co-op has become politicized, with a radical board mixing political strategies with the price of lettuce. The school district, particularly, with its policies set by a board including radicals, has begun to lose the confidence of people around the campus. School administrators (whose budget is the highest per student in the state) can hardly be faulted for responding in innovative ways—e.g., the "alternative" schools called Black House and La Casa de la Raza—to a school population that is about 45 per cent black, 45 per cent white, and 10 per cent Oriental, Chicano, and American Indian. Yet the diluting of what was once a classic dedication to academic education has exacerbated the

erosion of confidence. Although Louis Zlokovich, an assistant in the superintendent's office, argued to me persuasively that a child could still get an absolutely first-rate education in the Berkeley schools, a different and not uncommon view was held by Sheila Johnson. "If I had children, I'd move out of Berkeley tomorrow," she said, and laughed wryly. "Like many academic people, I'm an elitist when it comes to education."

Berkeley isn't all that special. It's not a left mecca. People in other cities are also beginning to say, "Hey, we can take this town." And they have been calling me to ask me to come talk to them about how they can put it all together.

—*Representative Ronald V. Dellums*

As I suggested earlier, the troubles in Berkeley grow less out of what has actually been done than from the possibilities of what may be done in the future. Two significant straws in the wind became visible in the June, 1972, elections in which Mr. Dellums won the Democratic primary by an overwhelming majority over a white opponent who did not, in fact, have much going for him. The other straw was a rent-control measure that was, by all responsible accounts, badly conceived, but that won a substantial endorsement, particularly among the students, whose interest is understandable. If the youthful population around the campus can be organized again for the April, 1973, election, there is a real possibility —some people call it a certainty—that the new council will see a radical majority of five to four.

Predictions of what will happen then vary widely, and, I suspect, depend more on the speaker's temperament than on that least scientific of disciplines, "political science." Professor Paul Seabury has suggested that Berkeley may be plunged into disaster and chaos, and has written, "In microcosm, the fears and angers of a nation in cultural travail now are impacted upon a relatively small and, in outward

In an "alternative" classroom at Berkeley High School, opposite, students opt out of class activities to rest or observe from behind a partition. Responding to student unrest, Berkeley High School now consists of seven separate schools, one a conventional high school, which the majority of students attend, and six "alternative" schools. The students shown here attend Community High School, one of the alternatives. Another of the alternative schools is solely for blacks, another for those of Mexican descent. In liberal Berkeley, which prided itself on its integrated schools, such voluntary racial segregation is yet another blow to the old order and to its most cherished ideals.

respects, unpretentious middle-class community."

By contrast, Sol Stern, writing in *The New York Times Magazine*, has predicted that "in the next several years the council has an opportunity to make Berkeley a model for the restoration of community in our overpoliticized and bureaucratic society—and that may be the most radical thing to happen to Berkeley."

Ed Kallgren inclines toward the view that Berkeley is working its way through a difficult experience from which it will emerge a better place. Yet, he adds, "Berkeley *may* go down. It *may* be a traumatic, wrenching, disastrous situation—that's possible. For the old-time Berkeley residents, for the traditional residents, it *may* become an intolerable situation. This could be so within a year or two."

And so, at the end of this essay I am driven back to the point where I began. The air around Berkeley is indeed becoming less penetrable, and it is increasingly hard for me to tell what the time there really is. I feel obliged, however, to keep straining for a clearer vision, for what has been happening in Berkeley is surely going to happen in other cities. Berkeley is only, as it has often been, a few hours ahead.

Kenneth Lamott, a novelist, is a practiced observer of the Berkeley scene and acts as HORIZON's *old California hand.*

The Raft of the Medusa

Adrift in mid-ocean, 150 castaways struggled and died until only 15 remained alive. Out of a scandal that rocked France, Théodore Géricault created a pictorial "*J'accuse*" that was also his finest work

It is a colossal canvas, sixteen feet high by twenty-three feet wide, and if you stand fairly close to it, "you already feel as though you had one foot in the water," as Delacroix said after attending its debut at the Paris Salon of 1819. Unlike most of the overblown story-telling pictures of the epoch, its size is not in inverse proportion to its historical importance: indeed, Théodore Géricault's *Raft of the Medusa* launched the romantic movement in French painting just as decisively as Victor Hugo's *Hernani* rang up the curtain on the romantic theatre and Hector Berlioz's *Symphonie Fantastique* proclaimed a new age of romantic music.

Géricault, however, was a full ten years ahead of the others, which made his task correspondingly difficult and his leap all the more spectacular. His particular contribution to romanticism has to do with style and technique, but above all with the artist's emotional involvement as an *homme engagé*. His predecessors had painted beautifully affirmative pictures for the Church or the party in power—such as Jacques Louis David's neo-Roman portraits of Napoleon.

Géricault, who would have belonged to the opposition party no matter what the issue, chose to be a protest painter long before dissent had become a familiar and even fashionable way of art. He put fifteen shipwrecked men and four corpses on a raft in mid-ocean and held them up to view as an indictment of the crimes and blunders that were responsible for their ordeal. At one stroke he

Géricault drew this self-portrait at the time he was working on The Raft of the Medusa. *In the detail of the painting opposite, the castaways hail the rescue vessel on the horizon.*

realized all the rebel ambitions that the young painters of his generation had been talking about: instead of a classical subject, he was dealing with a current event; in place of stylized nudes, there were flesh-and-blood bodies in postures of suffering and death. If this was an allegory on the human condition, no wonder the critics accused him

of being a man without a sense of the beautiful.

When the picture was first exhibited, the catalogue, in deference to the censor, listed it simply as a *Shipwreck Scene.* But no one had to be told who these men were, or of what disaster the victims. The shipwreck of the frigate *Medusa* had precipitated a great political scandal, which the government of Louis XVIII had vainly tried to suppress. People saw it as far more than just a maritime disaster: it was symptomatic of everything that was wrong with the Bourbon Restoration and the émigré officials who flocked back to France after the fall of Napoleon. The captain of the *Medusa,* Duroys de Chaumareix, was an aristocrat of the *ancien régime* who had been a lieutenant in the navy at the outbreak of the French Revolution and had then gone into exile; he had not been to sea for twenty-five years prior to being appointed to his command. His frigate was the flagship of a small squadron ordered to Senegal in 1816 to take formal possession of the African colonies that the British had seized from Napoleon and were restoring to the Bourbons under the Treaty of Paris.

The squadron had hardly left port before De Chaumareix lost contact

By FREDERIC V. GRUNFELD

In planning his picture, Géricault wavered between various episodes of the shipwrecked men's terrible odyssey. The early sketch above shows the rescue; the sailor climbing into the boat is taken from a drawing by Michelangelo. Géricault's careful drawing at right is one of several based on an eye-witness account of the mutiny on the raft.

with his escort vessels. A few days later, on July 2, 1816, he ran his ship aground on a sandbank some seventy miles off the coast of what is now the republic of Mauritania.

The frigate was loaded to the gunwales with four hundred passengers and crew members, nearly twice as many as her lifeboats could hold. (In spite of what Buckminster Fuller says about the ingenuity of seagoing man being responsible for most of the world's technological development, sailors seem just as incapable of learning their lessons as the rest of us; cf. the *Titanic*.) Among the passengers were the newly appointed governor of Senegal with his family and members of his staff, two companies of soldiers from a battalion destined for service in Africa, and a large number of civilians, including twenty-one women. When the frigate ran aground, her boats might have managed to pull her off had the captain immediately jettisoned the flour in her hold, but this cargo seemed too precious to throw overboard. Then, when the ship began to be battered to pieces by the waves, the governor sketched out a plan for a raft to be used by the surplus people. All the available spars and timbers were lashed together to

form a makeshift platform 65 feet long and 23 feet wide.

At last, on July 5, the order was given to abandon ship. The ladies and gentlemen of quality embarked on the captain's and the governor's barges. Most of the naval personnel found seats in the four other lifeboats. That left 149 men and one woman, a sergeant's wife, to be loaded aboard the raft—an operation attended by the high degree of military efficiency for which troop movements are noted. In their hurry to leave, the ship's officers made no serious effort to provide this mob with anything to eat or drink; the castaways were sent off with only a bag of sea-soaked biscuit, two small casks of water, and (this being a French ship) six barrels of *vin ordinaire*.

With 150 people on board, the raft nearly sank under the weight. Everyone was standing in water up to the waist, and crowded so close to the others that it was hardly possible to take a step, let alone sit or lie down. Ropes had to be rigged to keep the men at the edges from falling overboard even in calm weather. A stubby mast was fitted with a small sail, but it was almost totally useless.

The four officers on the raft had all

declined opportunities for seats in the lifeboats. Among them were Alexandre Corréard, a civil engineer who had not wanted to abandon the twelve construction workers in his care, and Henri Savigny, one of the ship's surgeons, who had refused to leave these men without the services of a doctor. It was they who afterward wrote the grimly accusatory *Account of the Shipwreck of the Medusa*, which is our principal source of information about the disaster. The naval officer ostensibly commanding the raft was an expendable midshipman, Coudin, who had been injured in an accident and was unable to move his legs. His attempts to obtain charts and a sextant had proved fruitless, and when someone afterward managed to find a pocket compass, it slipped from Coudin's hands and was lost between the timbers of the raft.

Duroys de Chaumareix did not bother with the maritime protocol that the captain is the last to leave his ship; he was off amid shouts of *"Vive le Roi!"* while there were still seventeen men left on the hulk of the frigate. Most of them, admittedly, were men who had broken into the wine stores and were too drunk to care. The origi-

Ultimately, Géricault decided to depict the dramatic moment when, on the thirteenth day of their ordeal, the raft's few survivors at last sighted a ship. In this oil study for the picture's final version, one of the two that have been preserved, the figures are grouped in a line that begins at lower left with dead and dying men and rises to the right, to end in the men who struggle to their feet, pointing or signaling to the distant vessel. But these gesturing figures provide only a weak culmination to the upward thrust of the composition. It was after completing this study that Géricault was inspired to construct the human pyramid, with a black sailor at its apex, that dominates the finished painting.

nal plan had been for the lifeboats to tow the raft to the nearest point on the African shore. But the submerged raft proved too unwieldy for easy towing and threatened to impede the progress of the boats. Before long, to the horror of the men watching from the raft, one boat after another slipped its towrope, leaving them helplessly adrift on the open sea. A junior lieutenant in one of the small boats tried to protest when he saw a sailor on the captain's barge drop the line: "Captain, take your towrope again," he shouted. *"Oui, mon ami!"* was the answer, but the captain merely ordered his men to hoist sail and make for the African coast, which was, in fact, so close that it came in sight before sundown.

Savigny and Corréard later estimated that the boats could have towed the raft to safety in a couple of days. "Perhaps they would have been forced to forsake us the second night after our departure, if indeed more than 36 hours had been required to tow us to land; for the weather was very bad; but we should then have been very near to the coast, and it would have been very easy to save us: *at least we should have had only the elements to accuse!"*

The men on the raft were a cross section of the forgotten people of Restoration France: old soldiers who had fought for Napoleon and were now, for lack of employment at home, being shipped off to the colonies; convicts recruited for service in fever-ridden outposts; petty clerks, hospital attendants, construction workers, sailors, a twelve-year-old cabin boy . . . Standing there, unable to move, half in the water and half out of it, they suffered from a strange kind of claustrophobia amid an infinite expanse of open sea. On the first day, burned by the African sun and pounded by the long Atlantic rollers, they consumed their entire food supply, but for a time their main concern was simply staying on the raft. "In the middle of the night the weather was very bad; very heavy waves rolled upon us, and often threw us down with great violence; the cries of the people were mingled with the roaring of the billows; a dreadful sea lifted us every moment from the raft and threatened to carry us away."

The inevitable thinning-out process began that night, when several men were swept overboard and another dozen crushed to death by the constantly shifting timbers of the raft. On the second day, though the sea was calm, some threw themselves off the raft in despair; others began suffering from hallucinations. When a new and more violent storm broke that night, dozens lost their footing and were drowned. Many of the soldiers and sailors mutinied at the same time. One group fell on the wine casks, "resolved to soothe their last moments by drinking till they lost the use of their reason . . ." and in their drunken fury tried to kill the officers gathered near the center of the platform.

Soon there was hand-to-hand fighting along the length of the raft. "Every moment men presented themselves, armed with knives, sabres and bayonets; many had carbines, which they used as clubs." Corréard rallied the officers and his loyal troop of workmen in what was rapidly becoming a kind of mad model of the nineteenth-century class struggle: the rank-and-file plebs versus the officers and the clerisy. During the attack, the mutineers actually succeeded in throwing the water casks and two wine casks into the sea. By the time peace was restored, more than sixty men had been killed or washed overboard, leaving the survivors some much-needed room. And now they were only knee-deep in the water.

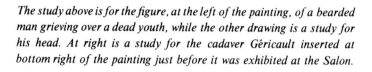

The study above is for the figure, at the left of the painting, of a bearded man grieving over a dead youth, while the other drawing is a study for his head. At right is a study for the cadaver Géricault inserted at bottom right of the painting just before it was exhibited at the Salon.

The mutiny had also solved their food problem, after a fashion. "Those whom death had spared . . . fell upon the dead bodies with which the raft was covered, and cut off pieces, which some instantly devoured." The officers, with their more delicately conditioned feelings, at first refused to touch human flesh. Instead they tried eating leather belts and cartouche cases. But on the fourth day they learned to eat sun-dried human flesh dressed with bits of flying fish that had got entangled in the raft. "We gave [ten or twelve] bodies to the sea for a grave, reserving only one, destined to feed those who, the day before, had clasped his trembling hands, vowing him an eternal friendship." Feeling their strength revive, the soldiers of the African battalion worked up to another outbreak of violence. "Soon the fatal raft was covered with dead bodies, and flowing with blood. . . ."

On the fifth day only thirty were left alive, but at least a certain *esprit de corps* began to make itself felt. On the seventh day two soldiers who bored a hole in the last wine cask were summarily tossed overboard (not eaten) by the others. Of those who remained, only fifteen seemed likely to live for some

days: the rest, ill or wounded, and obviously doomed, were consuming too much of the dwindling wine ration and taking up precious space. Instinctively, the healthy ones now chose (had they but known it) the Darwinian solution: if the fittest were to survive, the unfit — including the sergeant's wife — would have to be jettisoned, along with whatever remained of the Christian ethic. "So after a debate, at which the most dreadful despair presided, it was resolved to throw them into the sea. This measure, however repugnant it was to ourselves, procured the survivors wine for six days."

During these six days, still drifting aimlessly, they seemed to be coming closer to shore, for they saw birds and butterflies flying overhead. Finally, on the thirteenth day of their ordeal—the morning of July 17—they sighted a sail on the horizon. "The sight of this vessel excited in us a transport of joy which it would be difficult to describe; each of us believed his deliverance certain, and we gave a thousand thanks to God; yet, fears mingled with our hopes: we straitened some hoops of casks, to the end of which we tied handkerchiefs of different colours. A man, assisted by us all together,

mounted to the top of the mast and waved these little flags."

To their horror the ship suddenly vanished, and not until two hours later did they see her again, bearing down on them under full sail. "Saved! See the brig close upon us!" It was the *Argus*, one of the *Medusa*'s escort vessels, but of the fifteen survivors she took aboard, five were so weak that they died after reaching the port of Saint-Louis. Before then, they had the satisfaction of receiving a heroes' welcome from a committee that included the governor, the captain, and the other officers who had set them adrift.

Months later, Savigny and Corréard met again in Paris, where neither of them succeeded in obtaining compensation or acknowledgment from the Ministry of Marine. In 1817, after newspaper accounts of the disaster had been suppressed, they published the whole story in book form, and their sufferings became a *cause célèbre*. De Chaumareix was given a show trial and sentenced to three years' imprisonment. But public opinion persisted in laying the blame on the ultras in the government.

It was at this point that Géricault became interested in the case and con-

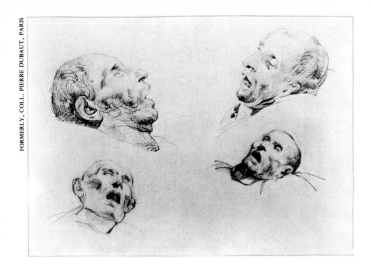

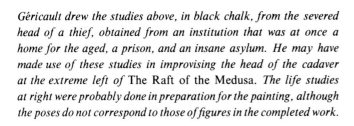

Géricault drew the studies above, in black chalk, from the severed head of a thief, obtained from an institution that was at once a home for the aged, a prison, and an insane asylum. He may have made use of these studies in improvising the head of the cadaver at the extreme left of The Raft of the Medusa. *The life studies at right were probably done in preparation for the painting, although the poses do not correspond to those of figures in the completed work.*

ceived the idea of painting a monumental morality-piece based on the incident. He was twenty-six, and had only recently returned from an exploratory year in Italy, where he had studied antique sculpture, Michelangelo's frescoes, and the painters of the baroque. He was a great lover of horses, and up to then his best pictures had been devoted to cavalrymen and horses. Physically he was the quintessence of the young romantic artist long before Chopin, De Musset, and Berlioz had established the prototype. "He was both impetuous and gentle," wrote one of his many women admirers. "Tall, serious, with eyes of singular beauty—dreamy, mild and profound, *à l'orientale.*"

Born in Rouen in 1791, Géricault belonged to a wealthy merchant family and lived in Paris like an aristocrat. The long, stormy love affair that he had been carrying on with the young wife of his maternal uncle, Caruel, was just drawing to an embarrassing conclusion: the aunt was about to give birth to her nephew's child. If he needed a pretext for leaving his house on Montmartre to avoid the family scandal, the *Medusa* certainly provided him with one. Since the picture he wanted to

paint was too large for his existing studio, he rented another in the Faubourg du Roule where he could set up his enormous canvas and shut himself away from the world.

Géricault approached his task with a documentarian's passion for detail. He not only read the book; he heard the entire story from the lips of Savigny and Corréard, whom he met through a mutual friend. They helped him track down one of the other survivors, the *Medusa*'s carpenter, who built him an exact scale model of the raft. To study authentic expressions of agony and despair, he went to the nearby Beaujon hospital. "There he found models who did not have to make grimaces in order to display all the nuances of physical pain or mental anguish, the ravages of disease or the terrors of death." The hospital staff also arranged to furnish him with cadavers and severed limbs, by-products of recent surgical operations, and for several months his studio resembled a charnel house.

Some of Géricault's most powerful studies in oil are compositions of miscellaneous legs and arms, or of guillotined heads: in one macabre canvas he combined the head of a guillotined

man with that of a young girl model who made the rounds of the studios. One day he met one of his friends, Lebrun, who was just recovering from jaundice and frightening everyone with his bilious appearance. Géricault took one look and was positively overjoyed. *"Ah, mon ami! que vous êtes beau!"* he cried, seizing him by the arm, and insisted on painting his portrait.

In the end it was the artist who triumphed over the documentarian. His central problem was the ancient and perpetually novel one of how to transform reality into art. In his preliminary sketches he wavered between several different episodes from the story: the first mutiny, the outbreak of cannibalism, the sighting of the rescue ship, and the actual rescue, when the *Argus*'s lifeboat reaches the raft. After many experiments he fixed on the critical moment that describes the horror and at the same time offers the promise of salvation. (There are, for that matter, a great many allusions here to the Crucifixion and the Resurrection as the baroque painters envisaged them.) This is the psychological instant when hope and despair are evenly balanced; it is almost as though he had wanted to illustrate, not the iron law of Darwin,

TEXT CONTINUED ON PAGE 32

29

In The Raft of the Medusa, *one of the most dramatic pictures ever painted, Géricault captured for all time the uprush of hope animating*

the raft's handful of survivors when, after unspeakable horrors, they sighted a sail. The colossal canvas is 16 feet high and 23 feet wide.

TEXT CONTINUED FROM PAGE 29

but *Das Prinzip Hoffnung,* the "Hope principle," which the philosopher Ernst Bloch has identified as one of the great themes of nineteenth-century social thought.

Once the subject had been decided, Géricault worked swiftly and with feverish concentration. He ate his meals at the studio, slept in an adjoining room, and even shaved off his hair to avoid the temptation of going out at night. Locking himself in, he began working as soon as the sun was up and stopped only when there was no longer light enough to paint by. No distractions were permitted; his assistant, Jamar, had to wear slippers in the studio. The only time he left his sanctuary was to make a quick sortie to Le Havre to study the sea and the sky.

The final verion of *The Raft of the Medusa* is an ingenious mélange of fact and fiction. Some of the faces and figures have been identified by Géricault's biographers: Corréard is the man whose arm points toward the distant ship, Savigny the one at the foot of the mast, the ship's carpenter one of those around Corréard. The Negro waving the cloth was drawn from a Paris model (Géricault shows three Negroes, though in fact there was only one among the survivors); Delacroix posed for the exhausted figure in the foreground, his head resting on the raft; and Jamar contributed the upturned face at the center. Despite the authentic touches, the composition is pure invention: to have shown the raft as it really was would have given the whole thing far too horizontal a thrust (see the oil study on page 27); instead, Géricault chose to build up a pyramidal structure, crowned by the brown figure against the dramatic sky.

It is on such points of order that the painter has to improve on historical reality. As Flaubert wrote about one of his own novels, *L'education sentimentale,* a work of art can fail by being "too true" to life. "Every work of art must have a point, a climax, must form a pyramid, or else light must fall on some point of the sphere. But in life

nothing like this exists. However, art is not nature."

How arbitrary this art could be was demonstrated just before *The Raft* was due to be shown at the Salon, when Géricault gave it a trial showing in the foyer of the Théâtre Italien. Only then, seeing it under an altogether different light, did he suddenly notice a great "empty space" at the bottom of his picture. Nothing daunted, he brought his paints and brushes to the theatre, called in a friend to serve as model, and added the dangling white-draped cadaver that completes (and in some ways dominates) the composition.

The Raft of the Medusa did not win that year's prize for the best painting at the Salon, which went to a Biblical

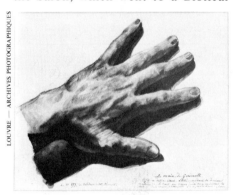

On his deathbed Géricault utilized the best anatomical model available: his left hand.

subject. Nor was Géricault's picture on the long list of those bought by the government for its permanent collections. He did receive, by way of recognition, a government commission to paint a Sacré-Coeur de Jésus for six thousand francs, an assignment that he secretly passed on to the impecunious Delacroix, obligingly signing his name to the result. Some of the critics liked his work, but tended to judge it according to the political prejudices of their newspapers. It was felt to be too large, or too ghastly; one of the reviewers said that he had slandered the Ministry of Marine. "But the wretches who write such stuff," Géricault declared, "have surely never starved for fourteen days, or else they would realize that neither poetry nor painting is able to convey with suf-

ficient horror all the sufferings which the people of the raft had to undergo."

Discouraged and depressed, Géricault accepted an invitation to show the picture in London, where it scored a major success in a gallery on Piccadilly, earning him nearly twenty thousand francs at the box office. When he returned to France, he was full of plans for other monumental variations on the *Prinzip Hoffnung:* the Greek War of Independence, the African Slave Trade, and the Liberation of the Prisoners of the Spanish Inquisition. But he was never to exhibit another picture. Already in precarious health, he was injured in a fall from a horse and developed a tubercular abscess of the spine. For the last half year of his life he was unable to leave his bed. When Alexandre Dumas paid him a visit a week before his death, he was making with his right hand a drawing of the left.

"What are you doing there, Géricault?" a friend asked.

"You can see, my dear fellow, I am utilizing myself. My right hand will never find a study in anatomy equal to that afforded by my left, and the egotist avails himself of it."

Dumas says in his memoirs that by then Géricault had become so emaciated "that through the skin one could see the bones and muscles of his hand, as one sees them in those plaster casts given to students." When he died, in 1824, leaving his worldly goods to his son-cousin, his executors had great difficulty persuading the Ministry of Fine Arts to buy his *chef-d'oeuvre* for six thousand francs. "As it was," says Dumas, "the Government only bought it with the intention of cutting out five or six heads, which were to be used as studies for the art pupils." The authorities were dissuaded in time, and *The Raft* floats on, majestically intact, in one of the great galleries of the Louvre, to remind painters that their rightful place is with the abandoned, the expendable, and the downtrodden. Only the paint is a bit cracked from having been rolled up for its voyage across the Channel and back.

An Inquiry

by various authorities into the dubious virtues and documented vices of

BIGNESS

Since the birth of the Republic,

one of our most cherished beliefs has been that

Bigger is Better. Now we may have to admit that

the giant economy size is not always economical

ILLUSTRATIONS FOR HORIZON BY TOMI UNGERER

A PLAGUE OF GIANTS

Is the Post Office efficient? Is A.T. & T.? The U.S. Army? Penn Central?
New York City? Perhaps what the modern world needs is *Smallness*

The director of a nursery school in New York wanted a particular brand of cookies for the children. When she gave her order to the wholesaler, he said: "I can't promise, Mrs. L. Since the company got so big, they've gone berserk. We can't get the cookies we want."

The director had come up against one of the most significant social and economic illnesses of our day: giantism. Like millions of others, she was beginning to discover that bigness is inefficient.

It is a surprising discovery. Most of us have been brought up to believe that bigness brings efficiency in business and government. The result is that most of us in advanced societies are, in the words of Dr. Michael Young, a British sociologist, "surrounded and controlled by impersonal, remote bodies—giant states, giant trade unions, giant corporations."

But now the belief in bigness is being challenged on all sides. Too many ordinary people have had experiences like the nursery-school director's. They have suffered the frustration of trying to correct the mistakes of some huge anonymous body, a company or a government. Or they have assumed that large organizations are needed to run the infrastructure of society and then found, as New Yorkers have, that the telephone system does not work and the electricity goes off.

What could be called a philosophical school of smallness is developing. Leopold Kohr, professor of economics at

the University of Puerto Rico, has been arguing for years that small economic and political units are not only more humane than large ones but more effective. He had a chance to test his contention when tiny Anguilla withdrew from a federation with two larger Caribbean islands and called him in for advice on how to survive alone. More recently, he has made the case for Welsh self-government in *Is Wales Viable?*—an appropriately small book put out by a small Welsh publisher, Christopher Davies.

But the most persuasive contemporary critic of bigness is Michael Young, one of the most original thinkers in Britain. Dr. Young started the British consumer movement years ago. He may be best known for his deceptively amusing book *The Rise of the Meritocracy,* in which he showed that those who rise on merit alone may prove to be just as intolerant as hereditary autocrats.

Right now, Dr. Young is working

for the development of neighborhood councils in the cities and towns of Britain. He explained why in a speech he made in the spring of 1971. We have accepted the price of impersonality in large entities, he said, because it permits specialization, such as the research department of a giant company, or the esoteric courses of study that only a large school or university can offer. More important, we were certain that size brought economies of scale. And so, Dr. Young said, "Whenever anything goes wrong, growth is the stock remedy." The ailing company is enlarged by a merger. Government ministries are combined into a superdepartment. Local governments are expanded to cover large metropolitan areas. Universities have twenty, thirty, or forty thousand students.

"Always, always in the sacred name of efficiency," he said. But the remedy no longer works. "There is hardly a large organization in the country which has not gone downhill over the last quarter of a century. Is the Post Office as efficient as it was? Imperial Chemical Industries? The British Broadcasting Corporation? The Royal Air Force? The University of London? The Labour Party?" Dr. Young added some telling American examples: the U.S. Army, the Bell Telephone Company, the University of California, New York City.

"Almost all large bodies," Dr. Young concluded, "have become

By ANTHONY LEWIS

afflicted by a new wasting disease, giantism."

Computers and other machines thrive on size, he said: "for a complex of machines, the whole may be greater than the sum of its parts. But for a large complex of people the whole has become less than the sum of its parts."

Why? To Michael Young the reason is obvious. In our century the ideals of human dignity, freedom, and equality have spread among the people of the world. There have been great victories for civil liberty and social welfare. Those are fine things, but they make large organizations hard to manage: "Bigness can only work if people are willing to accept orders coming from the top. This they are becoming less and less willing to do; orders seem to conflict with the old notions of human dignity in their new, even more individualist form."

Society today abounds with examples of people becoming less amenable to management from above. Just ask a college dean, or the industrial-relations director of a large company, or a union leader. The demand everywhere is for "participation." Behind that vogue word lies the enlarged sense of human dignity that Dr. Young mentioned. In an often hostile world, of superweapons and events seemingly beyond anyone's control, the individual wants a say in determining his own destiny. He is no longer willing to take someone else's diktat on how he should work or learn or live.

The leaders of big organizations have become aware of the problem, Dr. Young said. They have tried to secure compliance with their orders by increasing the amount of consultation. But that way lies inefficiency: "By consulting at every level, so much time can be spent in passing information up and down and sideways that nothing much else is done besides just communicating."

That is the heart of Young's explanation of why bigness no longer produces efficiency. Everyone who has worked in a large bureaucracy, or tan-

gled with one, will recognize the symptoms of giantism. But many will still find it hard to accept Young's cure: "Seize every opportunity to reduce the scale of organization. Make things smaller, not bigger, in industry and in the public services, and often efficiency as well as humanity will be enhanced."

Obviously, small structures tend to be more humane than large ones. The one-room schoolhouse, the family-run grocery, and the corner drugstore are on a human scale; those who are part of them know each other. In a small organization, moreover, everyone can feel that he is somebody.

But is smallness possible in the last third of the twentieth century? Or is it just an escapist dream?

Certainly there are escapist elements in the revolt against bigness. Young people who leave the metropolis to farm together in Vermont may enjoy the experience, but they hardly provide a realistic model for the millions of dissatisfied people in an urbanized and overpopulated society. Nor has Professor Kohr's Anguilla. The challenge is to reduce organization to a human scale, as Dr. Young says, within the reality of today's great agglomerations of political and economic power.

Michael Young thought it worthwhile preaching the virtues of smallness to his own countrymen, but the British have never worshiped size as we Americans have. Their country is itself so small, for one thing, and they have an ancient tradition of managing things through local committees and boards. London, often described as a collection of villages, is made up of boroughs that manage their own affairs to a significant extent.

The real challenge of the Young thesis is to the United States. We are a continental country and have long been proud of that. And we have glorified size: big business, Whitmanesque landscapes, even giant apples and strawberries.

"This country remains gripped by the myth that unless something keeps

getting bigger and bigger it is doomed." So said Anthony Bailey, who moved from New York to Stonington, Connecticut, and wrote an affectionate book about his new home, *In the Village.* He added: "In fact, the reverse is often true, as some magazines with millions of circulation are beginning to realize. It may be harder to stay small, but then the growth may be within."

The lesson is a difficult one for Americans. Two generations ago Louis Brandeis wrote about "the curse of bigness," but most of his liberal friends dismissed his thinking as anachronistic. They were sure that only centralized power and uniform federal programs could deal effectively with economic distress and social backwardness in a great sprawling country, could overcome the habits of lethargy and selfishness and corruption.

To be sure, state and local governments are often poor vehicles; we talk about giving them more revenue and responsibility, but they turn out to be the wrong sort of government in the wrong place. Yet we know that programs administered from Washington, however superior the motives and the qualifications of those in charge, lack a necessary quality. Reformers are therefore ready these days to tolerate more diversity, to let Pennsylvania and Idaho be as different as they really are. The challenge to political thinkers is to find ways of maintaining national standards where essential, while allowing more local control. And the same problem faces administrators in education, business, and all of life.

"We should all live in villages," Anthony Bailey wrote. This is not possible, but we need the equivalent of a village in the life of work and of the mind. We are learning that we relate more happily and more effectively to small institutions. And that discovery marks, as Michael Young said, "a great change in human affairs."

Though strongly in favor of village life, Anthony Lewis lives in London; he is a correspondent for The New York Times.

BIGNESS IN BUSINESS

Fire the vice-presidents, the secretaries, and half the staff; then pay the
rest to Try Harder. Such is Petrie's Law, and those who live by it shall prosper

True story: Once upon a time there was a small department in a large organization. It was a typical pyramid—a vice-president, below him a manager, a secretary for the two of them, and below that five workers. To mesh with the rest of the company, their work had to be errorless and finished by 7 P.M. It wasn't.

Here's what was going on. The workers would finish and take the work to the manager, who would make a few changes (otherwise what was he there for?). He'd send it to the vice-president, who would make a few changes (otherwise what was *he* there for?). The troops had learned that whatever they did they'd have to do over, so they were giving it a lick and a promise. Upshot: work finished at 11 P.M. full of errors.

For once, the traditional solution of adding more bodies was avoided. Instead, the vice-president, the manager, and the secretary were de-hired. The workers were called together and told how much was available for wages and salaries. "Consider yourselves a partnership," they were told. "Hire whomever you need, pay yourselves whatever the budget will stand, decide who does what job—and see if you can get the work done without errors by seven o'clock."

For a while work suffered, but one day it all began to come together. It turned out the partners didn't need anybody else, so they were able to raise salaries an average of 25 per cent (everybody got paid the same regardless

of seniority). They split up the responsibilities, named one partner to pick up the odd problems, and discovered to their amazement that they could come in at ten o'clock and still get the work done without errors by four. They're all having a ball, the rest of the organization is jealous as hell, and the point (five people in a partnership work a lot better than eight people in a pyramid) is in danger of being missed.

The first time I noticed the fewer-the-better phenomenon was in 1952. I'd been working as a security analyst in American Express's investment department, a group of twenty-one men and women investing several billion dollars a year of traveler's cheque float. Our leader was a bright young man with the big picture and a good sense of humor who was in the running for the top job in the company; yet all was far from well. Two of the best people were underpaid, dissatisfied, and looking around; we needed an additional

senior analyst and an economist. I knew about the unrest among the field hands because I was one of them. We put in the hours, went through the motions, but our hearts weren't in our work. We had jobs. We did what was required, didn't do what we didn't have to, and got our kicks on weekends, vacations, and after hours.

Unexpectedly our boss died, and the company, with that consistent irrationality I later grew to love, chose me to take his place. There must have been a shortage in the executive ranks of tall blond Princeton men who could hit the ball 280 yards off the tee, because that's about all I brought to the task.

Feeling not a little guilty, I called my first department meeting. Since we all knew each other well, it didn't take long to reach agreement on what needed doing. Where to get the money to do it was the stopper. American Express was a very rigid despotism, and amending the budget in midyear was unthinkable. The second meeting produced the answer: if we really wanted to be top-drawer, we'd have to give up our secretaries, typists, and file clerks in return for the new analyst, the economist, and fair pay for the rest.

The transition was accomplished gradually and without an increase in overall budget. What the twenty-one-man pyramid evolved into was a partnership of thirteen peers. My job as senior partner was to get us the tools we needed and keep the rest of American Express off our backs. The other

By ROBERT TOWNSEND

partners' job was to run the best investment operation in town.

Having no secretaries, the analysts wrote briefer reports and depended more on oral presentations. The finance committee welcomed the relief from turgid essays. Having no file clerks, the analysts did their own filing. They threw out 90 per cent of the junk the clerks had put in there just to be on the safe side, and found they actually saved time by doing a little menial filing every day.

All of which led to my accidental discovery of Petrie's Law of detumescent organizations: "Fewer people paid more tends to produce excellence at no overall cost except to the people who get fired."

It should be noted that Petrie's Law (named after Donald A. Petrie, my fellow conspirator) is applicable to the public as well as the private sector. In *The Foreign Affairs Fudge Factory* the late John F. Campbell gave us an apt illustration:

Ellis Briggs when he was ambassador to Czechoslovakia shortly after the communist coup d'état of 1948 . . . had been pestering Washington, without success, to cut his staff of eighty personnel . . . by half, down to forty. One day the Czech government, unaware of this background, declared sixty-six of the American embassy's personnel *persona non grata* and gave them forty-eight hours to leave the country. . . . to Briggs it was a blessing in disguise. "The American embassy in Prague then consisted of thirteen people," Briggs remarked. "It was probably the most efficient embassy I ever headed."

It works in the professions, too. I know of a legal firm built on Petrie's Law. There are no associates, no junior partners, no clerks. Nobody earns less than $100,000 a year. If the firm takes your case, it will be handled all the way by a partner. He does all the grundge work himself, so he knows what he's doing. If he needs specialists, he hires them. He's good. He enjoys his work. He doesn't waste time. Come to think of it, that's the basis of Ralph Nader's success. His projects are partnerships of eight to eleven people. Each project is housed in a different building to cut down on cross-fertilization, otherwise known as goofing off. It occurs to me that Nader may be the only man on earth profiting from the lesson Jesus Christ was at some pains to teach us: when you're starting an organization, twelve people is one too many.

Well, you may properly say, since it works so well, it must be just a question of time until all our big public and private hierarchies discover Petrie's Law and start making themselves smaller and better. Right?

Wrong. As a matter of fact, they're all headed in the opposite direction lickety-split. Everywhere you look the trend is toward more and more people paid just enough to get them out of bed in the morning—otherwise known as the Motor Vehicle Bureau Syndrome. Here is how you create that kind of organization.

Start with, say, ten thousand employees. Put them all in one building and divide them into departments. When communication breaks down, develop inter- and intra-office memo forms, job descriptions, and a police manual. When expenses begin to get out of hand, develop rigid salary limits and layers of salary committees. Develop purchasing forms and procedures so that it takes six months to get a desk lamp. When the best people get frustrated and leave, the salary limits will ensure that each will be replaced by a warm body. At this point, Leo Rosten's Law (second-rate people hire third-rate people) will take over. Soon you'll have sixteen thousand sullen timeservers, each bitterly resentful of customer intrusions, and bent on getting even with the company any way they can.

This miserable kind of organization has become commonplace because we've ignored Petrie's Law and fallen prey to its opposite—The Let-'em-eat-cake Law: "More and more people getting a smaller and smaller share of the pie eventually produces total catastrophe for everybody involved."

Most of our big corporations and public institutions are dead or dying pyramids. Like fish, they're rotting from the head down. Unlike fish, they can be revived by decapitation. The dead layer of top management must be removed and the remaining people encouraged to form an organism consisting of small partnerships—as few as possible, but enough to get the job done.

I can give you the key to organizational fun and excellence: it's Petrie's Law. But I can't unlock the door for you. I don't know how you're going to lop the top off your pyramid; how you're going to take power away from the privileged presiders; how you're going to get power to people in partnerships. That's up to you.

So what's going to happen to all our overstuffed organizations?

Not a blessed thing is my guess. And I'm not at all persuaded that's a mistake. American incompetence may be one of the best things the world has going for it. Suppose we had a widespread espousal of Petrie's Law. Productivity would go through the roof, and we'd bury the earth in automobiles, Princess telephones, frozen krinkle-kut potatoes, and peppermint vaginal sprays. Can you imagine, for example, how awful it would be if the Pentagon's weaponry really *worked*?

I think we should all relax and enjoy the twilight of our fading romance with BIGNESS. Why fight it? Much easier to open another can of beer, switch on the boob tube, and get really serious about turning our brains into cornmeal mush. That way we can pass the time until the moment arrives when, to borrow Kurt Vonnegut's image, the noble American experiment, unable to sustain its giant organizations any longer, turns its swollen green belly up and goes pop in the noonday sun.

Robert Townsend, the former chief executive of Avis, is the author of a slim volume entitled Up the Organization.

THE TALL BOY

Robert Wadlow didn't mind the jokes about the weather up there, but
there were worse drawbacks to being the tallest man in the U.S.A.

Alton, Illinois, a small manufacturing city on the Mississippi River twenty miles northeast of St. Louis, at dawn on the morning of February 22, 1918, Washington's Birthday. In the back bedroom of a wood-frame bungalow on Monroe Street, a son, their first child, is born to Mr. and Mrs. Harold F. Wadlow. The child, who will be named Robert Pershing Wadlow, weighs eight and a half pounds at birth and seems in every way a normal infant. Of normal parents, too. His father, a construction engineer for the Shell Oil Company, is 5 feet 11 inches tall and weights 170 pounds, while his mother is 5 feet 4 inches tall and weighs 140 pounds. There is no history on either side of anyone being unusually tall or overweight. In consequence, the Wadlows haven't the slightest inkling that, astonishingly, their newborn son will some day reach a height of 8 feet 11.09 inches and weigh 491 pounds, and thus be the tallest man of whom there is irrefutable evidence in the annals of medical history.

At first, Wadlow appeared to be nothing more than a robustly healthy baby, and when he weighed thirty pounds at six months, his parents were delighted rather than distressed. They still were not concerned when he weighed more than sixty pounds by the age of eighteen months. Though their neighbors frequently remarked on Robert's unusual size, the Wadlows inexplicably failed to measure his height until his fifth birthday, when they found him to be 5 feet 4 inches tall, the same height as his mother.

In September, 1923, clad in a secondhand suit that had originally been bought for a seventeen-year-old cousin, Robert trudged off to kindergarten. Anyone who was taller than his classmates knows how embarrassing it is to be the gawky giant of the class, and Wadlow was nearly twice the size of the other children. Nonetheless, he was remembered by his early schoolmates as a cheerful, good-natured, and bright student. One of the most prevalent myths about giants is that they are inevitably oafish simpletons, like Lennie in *Of Mice and Men,* but this certainly wasn't true of Wadlow: he had an IQ of 124, considerably above average, and for several years, until he grew so monstrously tall that going to school became an agony for him, he got good marks in class.

Wadlow was a popular student with both his teachers and his classmates, and in the seventh grade he was elected class president. After school, and in the summer, he spent a good deal of time reading, hiking with friends, or swimming at the local Y.M.C.A. Thus, despite his unusual height, Wadlow had a happy, uneventful, and relatively normal Middle Western boyhood.

As the years passed and he grew rapidly taller, Wadlow began to attract the attention of the press. Shortly before his ninth birthday he was measured in the offices of the St. Louis *Globe-Democrat* and found to be 6 feet 2½ inches tall. The *Globe-Democrat* ran his photograph on its front page, and it was reprinted all over the country. Within a few years "the Alton Giant" became, with Shirley Temple and Baby LeRoy, one of the best-known children in America.

In spite of his increasing fame, and height, Wadlow doggedly tried to live a normal life. He played basketball in junior high school, and to nobody's surprise was the high-scoring star of the team. Later, as his weight ballooned up to 350 pounds on a gargantuan daily diet of more than 9,000 calories, he became too heavy and lumbering to play basketball. Like most other boys his age, however, he collected stamps, had a *Saturday Evening Post* route, went to Methodist Sunday school, and joined the Boy Scouts. In July, 1931, when he was thirteen years old and 7 feet 3 inches tall, he was filmed by the Pathé newsreel cameras in his Boy Scout uniform and became internationally famous as "the world's biggest Boy Scout." In January, 1936, he was graduated with a C+ average from Alton High School and entered Shurtleff College, in Alton. He failed to do well in college, however, and dropped out after a single semester.

By that time, having reached a height of 8 feet 3½ inches, he was the tallest

By THOMAS MEEHAN

human being in the United States, and he found himself inundated with offers to make paid appearances at fairs, in parades, and on the stages of movie theatres. For years he and his parents had rejected most such offers, but now, perhaps because he had little else to do with his time, he began accepting them. In the next four years Wadlow traveled some three hundred thousand miles around the United States, Canada, and Mexico on public-appearance tours, turning up everywhere from the New York World's Fair to a state fair in California. He even did a brief stint with the Ringling Brothers Circus, appearing with them in both Boston and New York.

Until the last months of this period, Wadlow remained surprisingly cheerful. "I think folks would be a lot better off if they used their handicaps instead of fussin' about 'em," he said, pointing out with a grin that despite his own handicap, "I'm getting along all right." He made jokes about how he always gave his hand-me-down clothes to his father and how he was lucky enough to be able to peek into hotel rooms through transoms without having to climb up on a ladder. He often spoke of how fortunate he was, compared with his friends back in Alton, to have had the chance to see places like New York, Washington, the Grand Canyon, Yellowstone National Park, and Hollywood.

Wadlow liked being asked for his autograph, being on the radio, and being the center of attraction wherever he went. Occasionally, someone in a crowd would make a cruel joke about his height, but Wadlow never let himself become upset. "Ninety-nine per cent of the people are O.K.," he remarked, "the other one per cent are just plain ignorant, so why should I let them worry me?" He met all sorts of famous people, including Jack Benny, Primo Carnera, Milton Berle, Maureen O'Sullivan, New York's Mayor La Guardia, and the governors of a number of different states. In Baton Rouge the state legislature made him an hon-

orary citizen of Louisiana, and in the state of Washington he dined with the governor.

At the time Wadlow appeared with the Ringling Brothers, in the spring of 1937, he was 8 feet 5½ inches tall, weighed 480 pounds, and was still growing. Earlier, when he was twelve, doctors in St. Louis had diagnosed his problem as an acute case of hypertrophy of the pituitary gland, and agreed that he would probably never stop growing until part of the gland was removed. This operation, they admitted, could easily prove fatal, so Wadlow's parents refused to let them perform it. (By that time, the Wadlows had four other children, two girls and two boys, all normal-sized.)

By his twentieth birthday, when he was 8 feet 6¾ inches tall, Wadlow's step had slowed to an elephantine shuffle. He was infuriated now by those self-styled comedians who several times each day asked him, "Hey, big boy, how's the weather up there?" And getting from place to place became an increasing problem. Before, he had done most of his long-distance traveling by train, but he could finally fit into neither Pullman berths nor drawing rooms, and so he took to the airlines. At Newark Airport, however, on his way home from an appearance on Ripley's "Believe It or Not" radio program, he accidentally put an elbow through the window of a TWA plane, and as a re-

sult, the passengers had to switch to another plane. Wadlow was so upset by this that he began to avoid flying; instead, he made even his longest journeys crouched on the seatless back floor of a seven-passenger limousine driven by his father. Earlier, when he had arrived at an airport or train station, he had had to get to his hotel either by straddling the roof of a taxicab or riding in the back of a truck.

Everywhere Wadlow went, a Gulliver among the Lilliputians, everything was ludicrously small for him—cars, elevators, bathtubs, shower stalls, toilets, and just about anything else one can think of. Unless it had been made especially for him, he could not sit in a chair without breaking it, and in hotels he had to put two double beds side by side to sleep. Sometimes the beds gave way beneath his weight, and he ended up sleeping on the floor.

For most of his life Wadlow had been remarkably healthy, but by the time he was twenty-one he had grown so tall, 8 feet 8¼ inches, that his body began to fail him. Among other troubles, he lost all sensation in his legs below the calf, and had to wear metal braces. In early July of 1940, not long after he had again been measured and found to be 8 feet 11.09 inches tall, Wadlow drove with his father to Manistee, Michigan, where he was scheduled to appear in a Fourth of July parade. On the afternoon of July 4, 1940, he suddenly developed a fever and doctors from the Manistee Hospital discovered that he had a serious infection in his left ankle caused by the rubbing of a badly fitted brace. Anyone else would have felt the pain days earlier, but Wadlow, having no feelings in his lower legs, had not become aware of the infection until it was dangerously advanced. Thus, at 1:30 A.M. on July 15, 1940, at the age of twenty-two, Robert Pershing Wadlow died in Manistee, Michigan, the victim of a bizarre side effect of his incredible height.

Thomas Meehan, just under six feet tall, is a succinct observer of the current scene.

WIDE WORLD

At eighteen, Robert Wadlow—8 feet 3½ inches—towered over his normal-sized family.

39

TOO BIG

Nonstop pop: *F-111* by James Rosenquist is eighty-six feet long—thirteen feet longer than the fighter-bomber it is named for. Rosenquist began his career as a billboard painter in New York City's Times Square.

Gulf Oil Company's giant tanker carries 2½ million barrels of oil, enough to befoul between eighteen and thirty-five miles of shoreline if the ship should ever founder.

"Mother's life seems just as fantastic to me as it must to everyone else," says Elizabeth Taylor's son Michael Wilding. "I just don't dig all those diamonds." Sixty-nine carats are shown in the picture above.

This giant earth mover, property of the Hanna Coal Company, Inc., devours two hundred tons of the Ohio countryside in one bite in order to get at the soft coal underneath.

A three-pound tomato: "Why then, can one desire too much of a good thing?" —*As You Like It*

About 125 acres of pine trees, like this stand in Alabama, are chewed up to provide us with one Sunday edition of *The New York Times*, America's strongest journalistic voice of conservation.

The biggest Presidential library yet is LBJ's vast pile in Austin, which costs the public more than $540,000 a year. It could house everything his thirty-five predecessors wrote.

Ayn Rand's delight: Hailed by its proponents in 1951 as a veritable model of public housing, St. Louis's gigantic Pruitt-Igoe Project turned out to be a dirt-ridden, crime-ridden disaster. In 1972, in the hope of making it more manageable, city authories blew up part of it.

American way of death: Long "double-bottom" trailer trucks like this one are still legal in thirty-four states. Motorists sometimes succeed in passing them.

Miles of files: If you are one of the "innumerable" individuals on whom the FBI keeps tabs, watch out. They can dig out your record, actual or alleged, before you can manage to say "Jack Anderson."

One-hundred-sixty-four-pound pumpkin: "You never know what is enough unless you know what is more than enough."
—William Blake

Effluence of affluence: This middle-class New York City family of five saved their garbage for one week. It added up to 107 pounds.

Not content that one World Trade Center tower would have been the tallest building in the world, the Port of New York Authority built two of them. Planned to draw 300,000 people a day to overcrowded lower Manhattan, the center contains one hundred more acres of occupiable space than the Pentagon does.

Colossus of Roads: The Federal Highway Administration has financed more than 255,000 miles of pavement since 1956, at a cost to the public that is seldom in excess of $40,000,000 a mile.

Spaced-out: On Atlantic runs in the first four months of 1972, Boeing 747's carried an average of 134 passengers in 490 seats.

> Stockholders also rejected a proposal by Mr. Gilbert to limit an executive's total annual compensation to $350,000. Mr. Geneen's salary and bonus last year totaled $812,494.

That's a lot of cabbage, but then, President Harold Geneen of ITT has lots of shredders.

Thirteen-inch carrot: "Give me excess of it . . ."
—Twelfth Night

The mountain labored: The forty people photographed above, and twenty others, spent three weeks producing a sixty-second television commercial—for a tablet designed to combat bad breath.

Super-duper-chief: The proposed memorial to Chief Crazy Horse will be taller than the Washington Monument. All the nearby Mt. Rushmore heads could be hidden behind Crazy Horse's.

The strip mine in the foreground supplies the Four Corners power plant (rear) in New Mexico with the twenty-five thousand tons of coal it burns daily—fouling the desert air for thousands of square miles.

BIGNESS IN GOVERNMENT

What happens when one agency sets out to build an airplane runway
on the same spot where another agency is laying down a highway?

A few years ago the adminstrators of the St. Louis airport decided they needed a longer runway to handle increasing jet traffic. At the same time, the Missouri State Highway Department was planning a new freeway. Sustained by large grants from separate divisions of the federal Department of Transportation, two teams of draftsmen set to work. Not until their respective plans were submitted to a federal-state clearinghouse was an unfortunate overlay discovered: the new highway was to slice across the new runway.

For once, that overfunded technological juggernaut, the federal highway program, was slowed down, or rather, deflected (the road was rerouted)—but only by a collision with another government agency. This is maddeningly symptomatic of the institutional conflict of interests built into an administrative system that has allowed, at last count, more than eighty-one thousand separate governmental units to spawn across the United States. Of these, the federal government itself is simply the largest and most complex; as the chief dispenser of funds, it is also the principal cockpit of competing interests.

The public welfare is not necessarily the prime beneficiary of these funds. The American way of spending sustains business by helping it capitalize its

profits and socialize its losses. Justifying relief expenditures to a 1936 campaign audience, Franklin D. Roosevelt remarked: "You know how many of these dollars have finally come [here] to the city of Detroit in the purchase of automobiles." The political rhetoric of this policy became perverted to its essential rationale. The skewed statism that was good for General Motors was found to be good for the rest of the country.

Over the years, businessmen, farmers, and other special interest groups—from homeowners to beekeepers, and finally the poor and disadvantaged—competed for federal favors, until now a Congressional study has identified a profusion of cash subsidies, tax breaks, low-cost loans, and services in kind totaling $70 billion annually. "These programs are like Christmas, with everyone giving subsidies to everyone else, and Congress serving as Santa Claus," complained Senator William Proxmire.

The giveaways include tax breaks to suburbanites who inadvertently promote urban sprawl, and subsidies to builders to attract people back to the cities; they include appropriations for dams to enable certain farmers to grow crops in the desert, and subsidies to induce other farmers not to grow the same crops on the prairie. The study does not even attempt to assess the cost to consumers in the price protection of favored commodities at a time when the government is supposed to be fighting inflation.

In their almost pathetic eagerness to oblige the clients crowding around with Congressional blessings, many government agencies have distorted their original purpose out of all recognition, and in so doing have gone against the most elemental notions of what constitutes the common good.

Item: the Interstate Commerce Commission, responding to pressure from shippers whose complaints against the railroad robber barons originally brought it into being, set freight rates for raw materials low. Result: freight rates for scrap of all sorts are so high as to make recycling on a large scale unprofitable.

Item: the Tennessee Valley Authority, once hated by the private utilities as a producer of public power at low

By LAWRENCE MALKIN

"yardstick" prices, now supports a New South industry based on cheap power. Result: the TVA is the largest buyer of cheap coal strip-mined by a process that has raped the landscape and destroyed the culture the TVA was originally formed to conserve.

Of all the commodities protected by political clout, none is more notorious than oil. What is less well known is that the arguments for this protection have proved false. The depletion allowance was supposed to stimulate exploration, yet the amount of time put in by seismographic crews in the field, a gauge of oil-hunting activity, declined in the 1960's to half of what it was in the 1950's. Oil import quotas, which cost Americans $5 billion a year in higher prices, are traditionally justified by the country's defense needs; yet almost every drop of oil used by U.S. forces in Vietnam originates in the Middle East. Special exemptions have resulted in a particularly mad roundabout at Brownsville, Texas, where Mexican oil arrives by ship from Veracruz. Because of a quota exemption for foreign oil imported overland, the oil is pumped ashore and into trucks, driven back across the Mexican border, and then returned by truck to Texas.

Perhaps the most crowded trough of federal funds is the Colorado River basin, where for half a century Arizona and California farmers fought over irrigation water. But Wayne Aspinwall, the Colorado congressman who heads the House Interior Committee, insisted that the farmers of his home state get their share first. And so they did, through the Upper Colorado River Basin Project. With the completion of the Arizona irrigation project downriver, the concentration of salts in the lower Colorado increased to dangerous levels; Mexican farmers farther downstream, whose right to river water is guaranteed by treaty, have complained that it kills their crops, as the president of Mexico informed President Nixon last year. The river water will now be desalinated at government expense by pumping ground water out of artesian wells in

Arizona. That the wells could have been used for irrigation in the first place seems to have escaped notice.

Charles Schultze, a former Budget Director, calculates that it cost the government an average of $122,000 *per farm* to open newly irrigated lands in the 1960's. The expense of this program in some parts of California would make even the Pentagon blush: savings to the average California cotton farmer from cheap irrigation water and high cotton subsidies (and the cost thereof to the government) come to about seventy thousand dollars per year. It would be cheaper for the government to buy out the farmers at a lifetime annuity and let the land revert to desert.

Schultze points out that the price the public is willing to pay for this absurdity says something about social values: "The subsidy cost of placing one low-income family in decent housing averages about $800 a year. In terms of tradeoffs, therefore, the continuation of irrigation and commodity subsidies implies that public policy considers the maintenance of this particular farm in irrigated cotton production to be worth the placing of 90 low-income families in decent housing." The tradeoff can also be worked in reverse. A fair proportion of those low-income families need public housing because they were thrown off cotton farms that had been mechanized with subsidies. It would have cost the taxpayers—and society in general—far less to have subsidized them directly and left them on their small farms.

But government spending does not guarantee that the needs of the poor will be met. The Great Society programs of the 1960's were oversold and overfunded—and their cost has nevertheless risen by almost $35 billion in a decade. Ten areas were considered for the first Model Cities program, but no congressman wanted his district stinted, and the money was thinly spread over 150 cities. The same fate awaited the education program aimed at urban ghettos; expanding coverage in the city

of Washington, for example, lowered per-pupil expenditures to eighty dollars, hardly enough to make a difference.

Once in operation, government programs develop a life of their own. When Deputy Space Administrator George M. Low was asked to justify proposed billion-dollar outlays for a space shuttle, he replied: "The basic premise . . . is that the U.S. should and will continue to have an active space program from now on." In plain English, Low was saying that the space program had to continue because it was there.

The United States has backed into big government almost by accident, without any controlling tradition of a public will. The logical place for the expression of that will would be the federal budget, but on neither the spending nor the revenue side is the budget oriented toward any coherent plan. Instead, it is geared to the demands of competing claimants. Spending programs have been cemented so firmly into the budget that the government's official term for those that cannot be changed without Congressional action is "uncontrollable." These programmed uncontrollables eat up 71 per cent of the current $250 billion budget. And the process of simultaneously paying off both Peter and Paul has left the nation in such a fiscal squeeze that even when the economy returns to prosperity, the budget deficit is still projected at about $24 billion.

Until the 1920's the federal government did not even have a unified budget: spending requests went directly from the departments to Congress, and that symbiotic relationship persists between the government and its special clients. "It took them years to dig their particular tunnel into the public vaults," says former HEW secretary John Gardner, "and they don't want the vault moved." But some of those tunnels will have to be sealed up if we are not to suffocate in our own largesse.

Lawrence Malkin, a member of Time's *Washington Bureau, keeps his eye on the budget and other national monstrosities.*

BIGNESS IN SCIENCE

The scientific Hedgehog can find out something with his
millions of dollars and tons of steel, but the scientific Fox
may make a bigger catch while gazing into a fishing stream

The Fox Knows Many Things,
But The Hedgehog Knows One Big Thing.

So wrote an ancient Greek writer. For the past two thousand years men have puzzled about the inner meaning of this curious remark. The Hedgehogs of science certainly know a big thing— money. The situation is summed up in the following table:

PROJECT	COST ($)
Trip (round) to Moon	Billion (several)
Particle Accelerator	Hundred Million
Astronomer's Telescope	Ten Million

All of the rest—all of chemistry and biology—is mere "tiddler's stuff," as is said by the committees that award these vast sums to tough-minded Hedgehogs, Hedgehogs who know exactly what they want and will see you in hell in short order if they don't get it.

Many questions suggest themselves. Is the outlook of the Hedgehog necessary? Is it ironic? Is it bad? Strangely enough, the answers are probably all affirmative. The hardest question is the first one, the easiest the last; so I will tackle them back to front.

First, let me dispose of an argument against big spending in science that I do *not* accept. It is often said that we cannot afford such expenditures, that the sums involved would be better spent otherwise—pollution and the

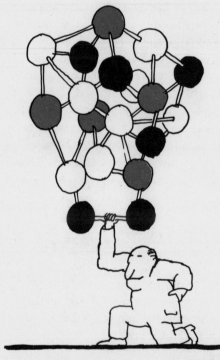

environment and all that. This argument seems to me a poor one. I believe there is no better purpose to which a society can devote excess economic capacity than to the investigation of the world in which we are living, the world to which we owe our existence. Our society possesses considerable excess economic capacity. We spend more in swilling beer and in maintaining a bloated gambling industry than we do on science. Expensive as the Apollo program has been, it is still

much less costly than the abortive war in Vietnam.

Nor do I accept the emotional overtones of the pollution argument. Pollution arises from greed. Antipollution, as it is currently understood, represents an increase, not a decrease, in greed. People want pollution removed without giving up the source of the pollution. The people of Los Angeles want their smog removed without giving up their cars. There is little worthwhile in this position.

The current argument against big spending in science is that science itself has become distorted thereby. The descriptions "big science" and "little science" are names that have arisen naturally from the equivalences:

Big Science = science involving big spending
Little Science = science involving small spending

Unfortunately, these valid equivalences have all too easily become replaced by the invalid equivalences:

Big Science = science involving the most important issues
Little Science = science involving comparatively unimportant issues

The Apollo program bears so meagerly on really important scientific issues

By FRED HOYLE

that it is tempting to use it as a monumental example of this kind of distortion. But the Apollo program is a sitting duck in this respect. The critical issue is whether projects like the particle accelerator in Batavia, Illinois, can be said to be concerned with deeper scientific questions than those that arise in little science. Most workers in big science argue affirmatively here, with more assurance, I think, than the facts warrant.

Recently I saw an ingenious experiment being put together in the physics laboratory at Glasgow University. The experiment was costing something on the order of ten thousand dollars, emphatically little science. It was concerned in confirming or denying the claimed existence of intense gravitational waves from the center of our galaxy. A positive result would rank as the scientific equal of a positive result from one of the main experiments to be attempted with the Batavia accelerator (the intermediate vector boson and its mass). Yet the cost ratio is ten thousand to one.

The case for big science must rest on two requirements being genuinely satisfied. The science must have a deep and lasting quality, and the results must be such that they could not have been obtained in a less costly way. The case for big science is frequently confused by false claims made in regard to one or the other, or both, of these requirements. Unfortunately, grandiose claims are difficult to refute quickly, especially if the claimant possesses a formidable public relations department. Certainly time itself eventually separates the wheat from the chaff—but by then the money has long been spent.

Even so, at the end of the day there remains a hard core of results in particle physics and astronomy that are of lasting significance and that could not have been obtained by inexpensive methods—for example, the difference between the μ-neutrino and the e-neutrino. If we deny big science, these facts will remain forever unknown. If

we open the door to big science, we invite false emphasis and distortions of motive. The dilemma is inescapable. Big science means big administration. It means big numbers of people working on its projects. This, I am convinced, must weaken originality. I have the strong belief that the measure of inspiration displayed by a team of scientists is essentially independent of its size. One man alone can have as much of it as a veritable brigade of scientistants meticulously clocking into their offices each morning. It is better for a man to be sometimes away, into the mountains or down to the river for a bit of fishing, which is where good ideas are to be found; for good ideas, like fish, need to be tickled carefully.

I remember glimpsing something of the excitement of Sir Ernest Rutherford's laboratory at Cambridge University. As a young student in the 1930's I used to tiptoe past it perhaps half a dozen times in the week. In those golden-age days, with no pressure from big budgets, no pressure of public relations, no need to give first priority to the writing of quarterly reports, young men turned up eagerly in the morning because they *wanted* to be there, not because they were required to be there. They knew, with good reason, that great discoveries lay around every corner and over every hilltop.

By understanding that the case for big science is always overstated, it should be possible at least to moderate the situation. Unfortunately, good intentions in this respect tend to be canceled by politicians and administrators who are more at ease with our scientific Hedgehogs than they are with the supporters of little science. The projects of little science are usually too slender and subtle to attract their attention, and are therefore dismissed as "piddling." Your solid administrator likes to get himself huge lumps of steel for his money, something thoroughly visible, no monkey business. Indeed, the Hedgehogs would very likely have an easier time of it politically if they could

somehow manage to make big science bigger yet.

So far I have said nothing about Foxes. In science we have Foxes in plenty, and they enter the picture in the following marvelous way. Our Hedgehog, bent on an enormous new project, must spend year after year battling layer upon layer of committees. Often enough, we have two Hedgehogs peddling different projects, confronting each other with argument and counterargument like Homeric warriors with shield and spear.

After years and years of infighting, our particular Hedgehog, victorious at last in committee, gets down to the nitty-gritty of constructing the huge instrument on which his heart is so unswervingly set. A vast tonnage of steel must be acquired and must be planed and honed down to the last thousandth of an inch. Years, many years, again roll by, with our now aging Hedgehog dragging himself wearily each dawn from home to office. Desperately he hangs on, determined, as he says himself, "to see it through." And so he does, until the day of the dedication. Then, that very night, even as he pours himself a self-congratulatory Scotch and soda, our Hedgehog collapses, worn out by committees, by money (inevitably the cost of his project has escalated), and by the sheer weight of steel. It is precisely at this moment that the Fox steps in. After giving our Hedgehog a decent burial, the Fox takes over.

This is the way of it in science. The Hedgehog thinks big and spends big, while the Fox sits by watching and biding his time until the Hedgehog's project is finished. Then, fresh as a daisy, the Fox steps in and cleans up the worthwhile science. It is just because it is this way that science is so healthy and flourishing. Even if everything else in our society should fall apart, the Foxes will see to it that science continues to remain this way.

Sir Frederick Hoyle is a noted authority on the biggest thing of all: the cosmos.

BIGNESS IN SCHOLARSHIP

How many millions of dollars and how many years (forty so far) should it take to produce how many volumes (thirty-four in print) on the life and works of an English literary dilettante?

In many authors, in many scholars, there is a touch of megalomania. Casting a jealous eye on the proud monuments of kings, they have dreamed what Horace and Shakespeare dared to boast aloud: that long after stone and brass have crumbled into decay, their words would still move the hearts of men. And the scholar, less concerned with hearts than minds, has secretly hoped that his life's toil would stand foursquare at the center of his subject, towering over the efforts of other men. But one perceptive essay, one brilliant article, or one small book is unlikely to remain dominant for long. So in scholarship bigness is all.

Think of the ancients, the hundreds of thousands of words in Herodotus, in Livy, in the multifarious works of Aristotle. True, a few, such as Thucydides, have been succinct, and time, which, *pace* Shakespeare, eats words as well as stone, has brought a welcome brevity to many an indifferent historian. But in general the man of many words wins. Gibbon runs to well over a million words; Michelet, Ranke, and Mommsen to far more. Even the lesser men, the Froudes, the Prescotts, the Bancrofts, have pushed themselves to produce and produce. But production as vast as theirs requires not only a natural ease of composition, combined with a hungry ambition, but also immense erudition, as well as temperamental stamina and considerable powers of physical endurance. So most

scholars hungry for immortality have found it easier to compile conglobulations of fact rather than write history.

In England, throughout the eighteenth century and into the nineteenth, country parsons and provincial scholars compiled vast local histories into which they poured all they could collect—inscriptions on gravestones, genealogies, manorial court records, histories of schools and chantries. Nothing was alien to their ragbag minds. Their names still resonate in the footnotes of learned monographs: Hasted of Kent, Ormerod of Cheshire, Clutterbuck of Hertfordshire, Nash of Worcester; though their books, huge folios running to millions of words, remain mere quarries.

Today, however, scholarship is no longer amateur. Scholarly gigantism seemed to be doomed at the turn of the century, when trained professionals began to replace ambitious amateurs. But hunger for immortality was too powerful to be suppressed, and some professional scholars continued to work in the old way—like Sir Arnold Toynbee on a great universal history that would explain man's past once

and for all. Others shuddered at so bold an ambition; their technique was to grab a small piece of territory, and, like the robber barons of old, erect a formidable fortress of scholarship upon it, piling monograph on monograph and defying their colleagues to attack. Unlike real fortresses, however, these structures were rarely rooted in rock, and frequently collapsed when some sharp-eyed scholarly mole undercut their foundations. Reputations formidable in their day crumbled into dust. The hunger remained, gnawing away: scholars yearned, as men do so often, after an unrepeatable achievement.

And they got it.

Not, however, in ways that might be expected. They were led to it by two rich collectors, both men of extraordinary character, considerable literary talents, and a capacity rare in scholars —administrative efficiency. In the 1930's W. S. Lewis first became interested in and then obsessed by Horace Walpole, the eighteenth-century letter writer and dilettante, and the son of Sir Robert Walpole, England's first acting prime minister. In his youth, Horace set out to mirror his age in correspondence with friends; between the 1730's and the 1790's, he wrote millions of words—not only in letters, but in journals, diaries, and commonplace books. In addition, he collected books, *objets d'art,* and trivia of every kind; although dispersed, these items were more often than not valued and pre-

By J. H. PLUMB

served. Lewis, a rich man as well as a distinguished scholar, set about collecting, not only Walpole's own letters, but also the replies. He also began to reassemble Walpole's library. Skill, ingenuity, charm, and dollars conjured up Walpole from the four corners of the earth; letters and books were discovered in Ceylon, as well as in Canberra.

But Lewis did not guard his treasure selfishly: scholars, bibliophiles, and research assistants were rapidly brought together, and contemporary reference works, along with microfilms of manuscripts, were assembled with astonishing efficiency and speed. Then the majestic volumes of the Yale *Correspondence of Horace Walpole* began to appear, beautifully and expensively produced, their print bold yet delectable, their margins as ample as an eighteenth-century palace.

And so, decade after decade, this enormous monument to Horace Walpole has grown as vast as the Pyramid of Cheops. More is now known about Horace Walpole than about any other human being. Lewis is a scholar with a capacious memory and a delicate sense of exactitude of fact, so his volumes are models of American editorial scholarship: nothing goes unillumined or unexplained. Here was, by its size, by the incredibly detailed nature of its scholarly apparatus, by its very completeness, an edition that could never be bettered, the cost of which could never be exceeded, one that must stand for all time. Hand in hand with Horace Walpole, Lewis has achieved immortality.

In Europe a second enthusiast, a scholar already famous for his bibliography of bibliographies, became addicted to Voltaire—another compulsive writer who lived to a ripe old age, leaving behind him millions of words in print and in manuscript. Theodore Besterman founded the Voltaire Institute, and by 1969 had produced more than one hundred volumes of Voltaire's letters and nearly seventy volumes of Voltaire studies. He has

since embarked on a definitive edition of the letters and has inspired a new critical edition of Voltaire's works; not surprisingly, his own contribution was the first to appear.

Yet these two gifted, rich, and effective men were but pilot fish to the whales that were to follow. Behind both Lewis and Besterman were massed small armies of scholars, research assistants, librarians, and secretaries, all as dedicated to their tasks as their masters had been. Before the mid-twentieth century their work would have taken generations, but modern business methods have swiftly translated their obsessions into realities. While most scholars are not rich men, they are often, in a quiet way, good politicians. They shrewdly took aim at a target that was both important and popular—the correspondence and papers of the Founding Fathers: Washington, Jefferson, Madison, Hamilton, Franklin—and teased substantial grants from Congress and the Ford Foundation. Both grants are now nearly exhausted, although the project is perhaps not more than half done.

The volumes, of course, are majestic when they appear. Take the Benjamin Franklin factory at Yale. The project started in 1954; but the establishment of editorial methods, the search for letters, memorandums, and the like, and the complex cross-indexing required by modern scholarship took time, and the fact that the first volume appeared by 1959 was something of a miracle. Since then sixteen more volumes have come out. Already, the grand design has had to be modified—résumés of less important documents are a slight retreat from the grand Lewis ideal of complete transcription. Even so, the edition, if achieved, will run to eighty or ninety volumes, and with luck may be completed this century, if. . .

And there lies the rub. Money. Each volume before it reaches the printers costs about $200,000, in spite of Yale's providing a great deal gratis; at present costs, the enterprise will eventually absorb some $15,000,000. And the Franklin factory is only one, though a huge one, of a score of scholarly enterprises that must devour millions in public, foundation, and university funds. Bigness, as Cheops realized, is always the easiest and often the most certain way to immortality.

But soon even these great editions may be outdated, for new historians are increasingly preoccupied with the computer. There is now a scheme afoot, if sufficient scholars and computer time can be secured, to reconstruct the population of seventeenth-century England from parish registers—an irresistible prospect to those suffering from scholastic gigantism. It would require hundreds of workers and millions of pounds, and lift historical research into the cost of middle-scale science.

For the foreseeable future, however, bigness in scholarship will chiefly remain the prerogative of the great correspondence factories—even though modern computer index techniques plus the Xerox machine have already made their methods as archaic as the illustrated missals of the sixteenth century. It would be much cheaper to set up a service for scholars needing the information than to print the volumes. But that won't happen; the swelling series, the groaning shelves, the meticulous performance of editorial tasks, afford scholars too much satisfaction.

Yet this trend toward bigger and bigger joint ventures is hardly new. The first two volumes of the *Acta Santorum* were printed in 1643; that project is yet to be completed, although work on it by the dedicated group of Jesuits known as Bollandists has been going forward ever since, apart from a break caused by the French Revolution. By the twenty-first century the entire cycle of the lives of the saints will probably be complete, but at that point a full-scale revision will doubtless be necessary. No mere secular enterprise can rival this one in majesty of conception; for bigness in scholarship, it must surely take the prize.

AHMED THE ELEPHANT

For millions of years, in the endless wilds, his size was his safety. But now
he eats out the whole understory of the dwindling forest. Next stop: the zoo

The largest land animal on earth prowls the bush in northern Kenya, near Marsabit, where, inaccessible to air-borne safaris, he may survive to his full span of about seventy years. His name is Ahmed and he is a national monument, so designated by the Kenya government. No one dares harm him.

Ahmed may weigh seven tons. His tusks may measure two feet around at the base and weigh two hundred pounds apiece. He is a dream, a fantasy in the flesh, for he represents man's infatuation with the notion that size has value and that, therefore, great size means excellence.

Ahmed may indeed be an excellent animal, and it is surely his size that put his ancestors beyond the reach of almost all hunters. Size gives him the strength of a bulldozer and a brain weighing ten pounds; size made him the once dominant animal of Europe, Asia, and Africa. Size enables him to shake fruit out of a tree, or knock the tree flat. He can pound a ramp into mud with pile-driving feet and, with friends, haul a stricken colleague out of a bog. He can swim submerged with his trunk held up like a snorkel. Size gives him a huge heart, a slow-paced life style, great longevity. Because he is so secure, he has developed a pacific way of life and intense, humanlike comradeship with his fellows.

Best of all, the elephant is adaptable, made so by a prehensile trunk that can lift and smash, suck and blow, dig and fondle. His tusks, his upper teeth, are the most dangerous natural weapon ever evolved. He eats hundreds of different plants, feeding on plums, figs, coffee berries, olives, butternuts, dates, celery, bamboo, raspberries, papyrus, and mahogany leaves. He is a seasonal party-goer, and with fermenting fruits or the buds of certain palm trees in his gut, he gets so crocked that his lurching, belching passage through the forest is a disaster for most forms of life.

But size creates problems for him. To sustain his bulk, he must eat at least three hundred pounds of fodder a day. His death rate is sixteen per thousand, but his birth rate is ninety. This is somewhat neutralized by his long migrations from one food source to another: from Kenya to Kilimanjaro, his migrant armies miles long, the rumble and roar of his hundreds deafening. On these marches, his young die. He contracts anthrax and lethal fevers, harbors ticks as big as strawberries and maggots that, tiny inside such bulk, can reach his heart.

Thanks to his size, he is not swift, so the first spear-throwers ran him down and caused fatal bleeding with jabs into the gut. They got him with poisoned arrows, with rock-weighted spears that plunged into his neck. They drove him over cliffs, or ringed him with fire and roasted him.

But these were mere pinpricks. Even the ivory-carving artisans of Egypt, five thousand years ago, did not much trouble him, though the Assyrians later obliterated him in Mesopotamia. A servant of Hannibal and the Romans, he was soon extinct in North Africa. But the continent is huge, and so is he.

The nineteenth century confronted him with a different challenge: he was suddenly out of scale, too big for the new world a-making. In fewer than a hundred years, five million tons of elephant flesh fell to hunters in the Congo alone. A quarter of a million tons of ivory from that region flowed into Sheffield (knife handles), London (billiard balls, piano keys), Dieppe (paper cutters, book covers, combs, napkin rings), Württemberg (ornaments), Bombay (trinkets, toys, models), and Peking (chessmen, puzzle boxes, curios).

His migration routes were cut by settlers. To cross East Africa, he ran a gantlet of rifle fire. Farms spread out over his feeding grounds. His giant feet and size made him easy to track. Muzzle-loaders once dazed or stunned him, but the new guns killed outright.

After this, irony. Men became alarmed. They protected him, controlled the shooting, established parks for his pleasure. His populations soared; he poured into the parks, the bullets of angry farmers and frustrated big-game hunters snapping at his hindquarters. And now he is, willy-nilly, an ecological disaster. He eats out the understory of forests and lets in fire. During drought, he develops an appetite for giant baobab trees: he eats the bark, the fruit, the leaves; an entire tree, weighing tons and perhaps a thousand years old, goes into elephant stomachs in one night. Over thousands of square miles, he may leave almost every tree felled, shrubs ripped up, the ground gouged.

So the men shoot him again. Now he becomes pet food and meat for hungry Africans. Some of his kind will have a few more decades of freedom in the Congo rain forests and in equatorial Sudan. About 300,000 strong today, he will survive in Africa, all right, but he is a mute reminder that in great size there may be melancholy imperfections.

In the Summer, 1972, HORIZON, *Franklin Russell wrote about the earliest ecological crisis of a smaller mammal: man.*

By FRANKLIN RUSSELL

Transports of Delight, and Other Contraptions

The great age of invention is not over: although his
fantastical engines may not impress the patent office,
William Crutchfield is a master at thinking them up

The old-fashioned goldfish bowl in *End Table* (above) might have come from grandmother's parlor. The little table is drawn with the precision of an illustration in *Popular Mechanics*. The rakish clipper ship harks back to the heroic age of nineteenth-century transportation, but the storm in the fishbowl is patently absurd. Such an odd combination of elements—the precise detail, the nostalgic rendering of objects and contrivances belonging to an earlier, happier day, the mock-heroism of imperiled ships in fishbowl tempests—these are the unmistakable earmarks of the work of William Crutchfield, aged forty-one, of modest renown, currently living in Los Angeles not far from the Sunset Strip.

Believe six impossible things before breakfast, Alice's queen advised, and Crutchfield seems to have followed that celebrated admonition. Born and raised in Indianapolis, home of the famous Speedway, Crutchfield lives by the proposition that man's mechanical feats in the period from 1840 to 1914 marked a true summit of human achievement and that these feats were nonetheless absurd. He loves the sheer bravura of steam locomotives, rickety biplanes, and oversized paddle boats. Yet his work is a devastating parody of the vaunting spirit behind them, the technological faith that holds that if a thousand-foot ship is good, a ten-thousand-foot ship is ten times better. Crutchfield is an artist who loves machinery and understands the fatuousness of this unrequited love. Some of his creations, droll, absurd, and oddly satisfying, appear on the following pages. —W.K.

Listing Tower *(water color, 1972)*

Second City of Troy *(water color, 1972)*

Outlandish marine architecture is a favorite theme of Crutchfield's. *Listing Tower* resulted, says the artist, sole authority in the matter, when medieval shipbuilders erected circular decks of stone before solving the problems of buoyancy. *Second City of Troy* is an ocean-going double side-wheeler that sank "about 1891." The magnificent sixteen-masted bark at right, *Eureka II,* fell to pieces off Cape Hatteras, reports Crutchfield. Rerigged, however, the salvaged bow portion became an American clipper ship.

Eureka II *(color screen-print, 1971)*

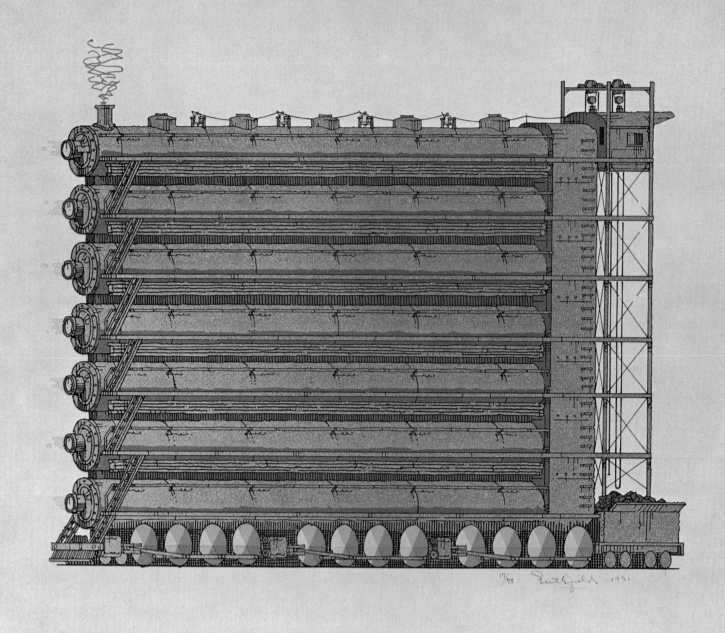

Six Rainbow Trains: Elevated *(color screen-print, 1971)*

PUBLISHER: BERNARD JACOBSON, LONDON; ABOVE: SAME

*I*n homage to the railroads, Crutchfield in 1971 created a series of "rainbow trains," vintage steam locomotives endowed with spectral hues. They include *Elevated,* the redoubtable seven-layered engine above, combining pulsating horsepower with harebrained design. Another "rainbow train" is the *Not-A-Train,* left, whose negative status is due, apparently, to the rubbery knot in its middle. It is often said, however, that man's greatest mechanical invention was the alphabet, a notion with which Crutchfield is in full accord. His *Alphabet Spire II,* opposite, is an Eiffel Tower of letters operated by a hand crank, as if the alphabet were literally a mechanical invention patented circa 1890, in Crutchfield's golden age of lunatic technology.

Alphabet Spire II *(water color, 1972)*

Six Rainbow Trains: Not-A-Train *(color screen-print, 1971)*

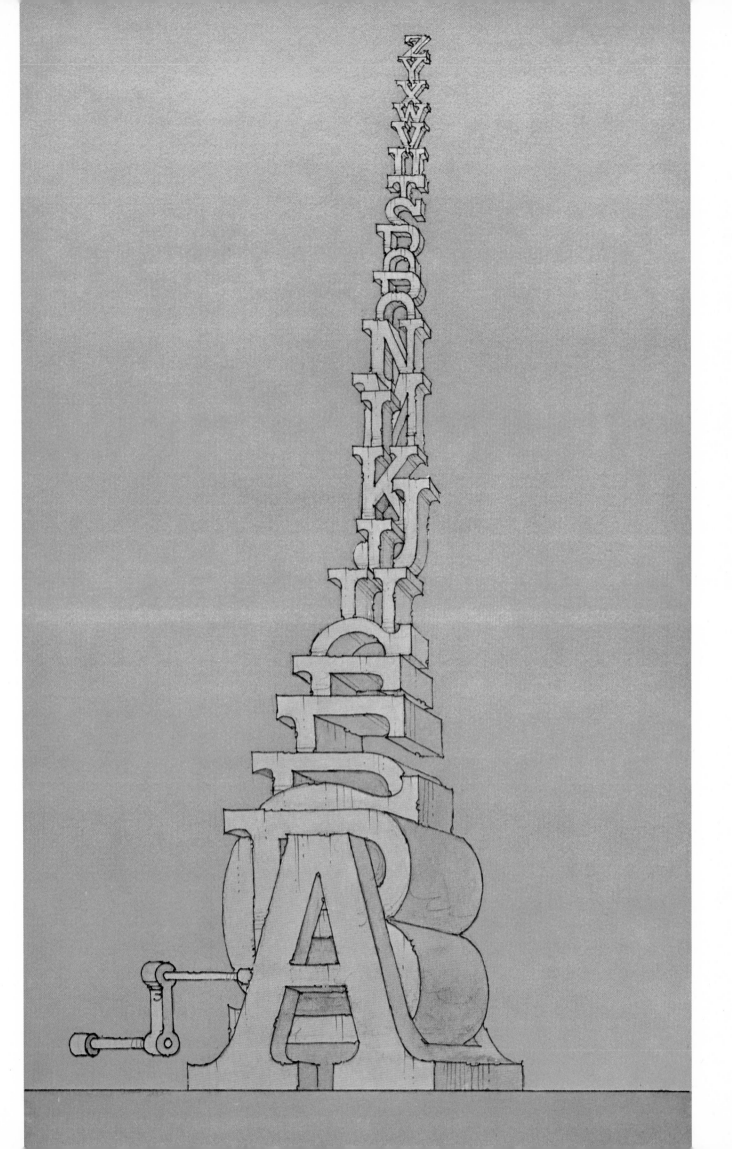

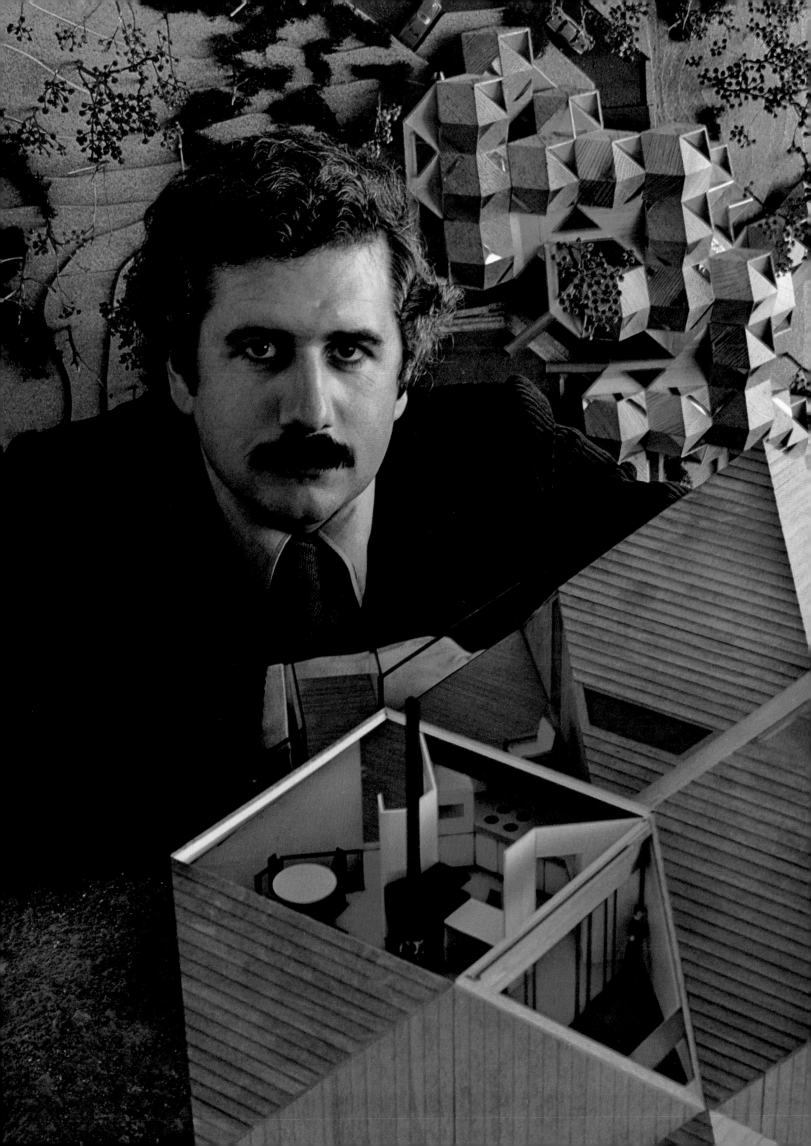

MOSHE SAFDIE

The young architect of Habitat says that what people crave is a "sense of house." He proposes to give them indoor-outdoor living, even in twenty-story apartment buildings

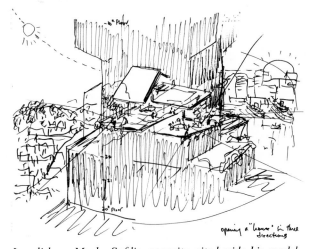

His life is a pilgrim's progress through Sloughs of Despond, across Mountains of Obstruction, finally emerging into radiant Valleys of Delight—only to be blocked there by Avalanches of Skepticism.

Can Moshe Safdie, the Canadian-Israeli architect who gave Montreal's Expo 67 its striking Habitat apartment building, negotiate every obstacle in his pilgrimage from current blight to future architectural glories?

"It really depends on the day I talk about it," he recently remarked. "Sometimes I feel we're on the verge of radical change in our houses and cities because the problems are defined and articulated, because technically we can solve them, and because things have gotten just bad enough for people to care. At other times—when I spend years trying to get a miserable 130 housing units approved and under construction in Puerto Rico—I get discouraged and cynical.

"The moments of optimism are much more frequent, but I'm certainly not as naively optimistic as I was in 1967 when I finished Habitat. It wasn't that I expected the world to come and see

Israeli-born Moshe Safdie, opposite, sits beside his model of a vacation-home complex for Saranac Lake, New York. Above, a Safdie sketch shows one way an apartment becomes a "house": by providing a view all around. The Safdie sketches on these pages were done especially for HORIZON.

and be converted—nothing so megalomaniac. I was in an optimistic mood because I tried to do something and I got it done, and that meant I could do other things. But some of my setbacks have made me more realistic."

In the annals of architecture, Safdie's accomplishment in Habitat will be an object lesson as long as men go on believing that wisdom comes with age. He was twenty-five and unknown when he set out to plan the structure—and he had never built anything before. By the time it was finished, in 1967, he was twenty-eight and celebrated, not only

as a practical man, but as a theorist who pointed the future course of urban design. He set down his thoughts in *Beyond Habitat,* an account of battles fought and won. In this interview he described his progress and theories.

"There's nothing revolutionary about what constitutes a good environment," he began. "It's been the same for thousands of years; a good space is a good space, and the fact that we can move into a house that was built a thousand years ago and feel that it's better than 90 per cent of the housing built today says something.

"The best houses I've seen or lived in myself have been Arab houses in old Jaffa, old houses in the old city of Jerusalem, and New England farmhouses with porches—houses that were designed for a different technology and a different life style, but which work very well today.

"It's true that the Arab house in Jaffa has more space than the modern house, but it also has things like a tradition of how a window—which is also a seat—happens in a wall, and the use of the wall to store things, and the possibility of manipulating the space by moving partitions. It has a sense of

Interior design for a synagogue in Israel

Model of a religious school, or yeshiva

what makes a space, with domes and arches and terraces extending indoors and outdoors.

"In our modern housing project there's a three-bedroom apartment of a fixed pattern—the corridor with the bedrooms, and a kitchen off the L-shaped living room. This forces you to live in a certain way, and you know, subconsciously, that there are ten thousand more people living exactly as you do.

"In the modern project you have the sense of a camp and regimentation, individual blocks which you have to find by looking up numbers; open spaces resemble no man's land.

"When you come along a 150-foot corridor, even if it's carpeted, and then up an elevator and out onto another long corridor, that does not give a sense of house. That's a sense of hotel, perhaps, or of some other transient environment."

Safdie calls a "sense of house" basic. He considers all his work on housing a matter of working out variations on the basic requirements of his own life, each variation responding not to how he thinks other people might want to live but rather to how he himself likes to live.

"A sense of house requires in the first place a sense of entrance—a certain ritual and event," he said. "Levittown has a better sense of entrance than an apartment building, because you first walk along a pathway and there's a certain in-between place before you enter the house. In Mexico you come into a court, an event between public and private.

"Contrast that with a thin door between a small public space which is a six-foot-wide corridor and a living room on the other side where you never really feel that you're away from the corridor."

Since Safdie likes space and feels most comfortable in large rooms, his sense of house demands the maximum of space. "When you have space you can be less specific about how it should be used," he said. "You can sit in one place and a week later decide you'd rather sit in another. As space shrinks you have to become more specific, until—in the extreme case—the bed comes down from the ceiling, and the desk folds up into the wall, and everything in the house becomes a machine.

"The home has shrunk because what we can afford to spend on housing buys little space. When you have acres of open space around, you can take privacy and a view for granted, and the space outside becomes an activity space.

"A sense of house means a feeling of freedom in space. If every unit looks three or four ways, so that you get a sunrise with the sun streaming in on one side, and then a sunset on the other side, and you see the river or the city, and you don't feel boxed in with a view only on one side, you begin to have a sense of house. If I sit at home and it's a sunny day and I can't sit among flowers and eat my breakfast outdoors, that's not a sense of house.

"I want to feel the weather, to feel the elements of each season, and I want a view because it's expansive, because it makes me feel I'm in a bigger space. I like the possibility of being outdoor-indoor, of making outdoor space usable, livable, and convertible—for example, by having a garden with a sliding glass roof and a transparent wall and sitting there in an instant greenhouse while there's snow outside.

"People live in quite different patterns, and they should be able to find appropriate spaces. There are families who would be happy with a very large space and minimal subdivisions, while other people couldn't stand to live that way. Some people have three or four

"Freedom in Space"

According to Safdie, a good building should provide a "feeling of freedom in space." The feeling is induced by imponderables such as sensing the weather and "the elements of the seasons." The apartment dwellers in Safdie's sketch, right, have an outdoor garden with a sliding glass dome that transforms it into "an instant greenhouse" in winter. Safdie's Yeshivat Porat Joseph, of which a model appears at far left, is now being built opposite Jerusalem's Wailing Wall. Its classrooms will have half-domes that open to the outdoors and rooftops that serve as walkways. In his synagogue, left, sunlight will filter through rooftop prisms, creating varicolored light indoors.

kids and eat every meal with them—the kids are always in the living space with the parents, and there isn't a feeling that it's necessary to be separated. Others want to be separated from their children, and then privacy has to be generated."

Safdie suggested that the ideal community would be a mix of families of different sizes, older people and younger people, married people and single people, parents and childless couples. He said that in each dwelling a family should be able to lead "a normal life" —which means that children would be able to shout while at play, and parents to argue on occasion without the neighbors listening in. Visual privacy would have to be assured.

Each child would have a private sleeping space (Safdie termed this "a North American criterion"). Children aged three to six would be able to move about unattended, and wander off fifty yards and meet at least half a dozen playmates their own age. For children six to ten there would be access to play areas within a space of five acres. Older children would be able—on their own —to go to movies, libraries, parks, and sports centers.

The difficulty about accommodating his personal preferences—and general-izing them to accommodate those of the public as well—is the density now imposed on housing. Safdie noted that we must try to construct houses approaching ancient ideals at thirty times the ancient density, and—as he said— "do it not only so that the sheik or the pasha or the landowner has the ideal house but so that everybody has it."

One trouble with this assignment is that, as he complained, people demand very little. When he speaks of the houses he would like to build, the reaction of his audience is that he is indulging in science fiction—that his vision is unattainable given current costs and technology.

"You have to expand people's expectations," he said, "because if you don't, they won't get what is possible."

That he is not talking science fiction is concretely evident in the Montreal Habitat that finally emerged from his original proposal for a cluster of 950 housing units in inclined rhomboidal planes leaning on each other, with pedestrian streets in the air and a complete commercial-cultural center below.

Because the Canadian government was unwilling to spend the forty-two million dollars Safdie estimated as the cost, his plan was cut down to its even-tual size and shape—a ten-story zig-gurat of 158 housing units.

The units jut forth like gigantic shoe boxes in the sky, as though waiting for the giant angelic hand that will shove them into symmetry. Each unit is made up of concrete modules poured at the site, with plumbing and electrical installations and windows set in place before a giant crane lifted each module and rested it atop another.

All the units have a view of the Montreal skyline and of the St. Lawrence harbor below. Each unit also has an outdoor terrace—with the terrace floor serving as the roof for the housing unit below. Instead of indoor corridors, there are aerial streets open to the air but sheltered from the weather. Each unit has a front door opening onto a street. What Safdie has produced is not an apartment house but a cluster of houses.

For a time the place seemed to be a white elephant. But then rents became competitive, and now Habitat is one of Montreal's choicest locations. Residents find that it lives up to the claims that Safdie makes for it—an extraordinary sense of privacy, a new feeling of space, a design for comfortable living in touch with nature.

When Safdie first proposed Habitat,

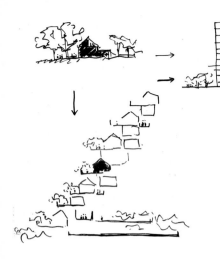

A Mountain of Cottages

The sketch at the left sums up in three related drawings one of Safdie's chief goals as an architect: to give apartment dwellers a cottagelike environment. No longer boxes inside a box, the apartments of a Safdie house are linked yet separate, with "private outdoor space for each family," a variety of views, entrances, and levels, and other essential features of "houseness." In his model for Habitat Puerto Rico, opposite, a structure for three hundred families looks like a complex of villas, and to a great extent it is.

and when it began to rise from the earth, people asked him what it was (since this was not clear from the unorthodox shape). He found himself replying, "It's a prototype."

"A prototype can show how to house people in a way which will enrich their lives," he said.

At that point in the interview, Safdie sat erect in the rocking chair where he had earlier settled comfortably, and became the man of platforms and methods —outlining a three-point attack.

"How do we build faster and cheaper, using better materials and better production methods so that we can make more environment and more house?" he began. "This is the most comprehensible level of action, because everybody understands efficient technology. If, instead of pouring concrete that weighs 150 pounds per cubic foot you have material that weighs 20 pounds per cubic foot, which can be molded to make any space you want and which is cheap and strong and has good thermal insulation, then progress can be comprehended.

"The second area is economic-political—how we spend our resources and energy. In the final analysis there's a limit to the miracles technology can perform. If we want a better city or a better house for everybody, we're talking about radical changes in the polit-

ical-economic system, how we spend our national and individual incomes. If the majority of Americans can't afford new urban housing—in terms of the cost of land, construction, and money —it has more to do with the distortion of the total system than with their individual incomes.

"And the third question is how we conceive, how we give form, how we design our environment. This is the least comprehensible, and the one that's normally taken for granted. Most people assume that if technology made the advances we hope it might, and if the political changes took place, we would have a good environment. Russia's society is the clearest example that an attempt to radicalize technology and the economic issues of environment does not of itself produce good houses."

Safdie believes each house should be distinctly different from all others, just as human faces and personalities differ from one another.

"When houses were made with adobe or stone or wood, by the nature of the material and the process of building you could manipulate them to be a little different every time," he said. "Peasant villages were systems with certain environmental qualities built into them."

Safdie suggested that the equivalent must exist for our twentieth-century cities: every unit should have outdoor space, gardens, and views open to sun-

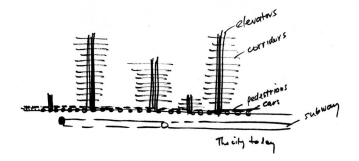

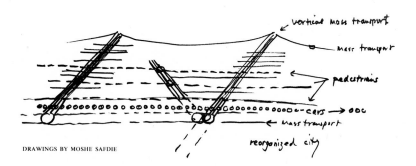

"The City of Choice"

The city that maximizes choice is, for Safdie, the ideal city, and "the key to the city of choice," in his words, "is mobility." In today's cities, as the sketch at left shows, the private elevator is the main vertical transport. In the "reorganized city" funicular mass transport would climb the city's man-made mountains; car-free walkways on all levels would enable urban man to travel chiefly on foot. Such mobility means a dense population, but since people would live in Habitats, every city dweller would enjoy seclusion at home.

rise and sunset. The private outdoor space for each family should be roughly the same size as the indoor space—even though it is on the twentieth floor (this requirement would make just about all contemporary apartment houses unacceptable).

In North America, at least, the ideal arrangement would allow one to drive a car into the kitchen. But within Safdie's "inner community" of five thousand people, pedestrians and vehicles would never intersect.

"How do you group units at the density of a building that rises twenty stories in the center of New York and give people the kind of flexible dwellings I recommend?" he said. "You work back from your objective to technology and say that one way would be to make a machine which works in a particular way, or to use a material which works in a particular way, or to manufacture space cells, parts of buildings, on a factory assembly line.

"We still build individual buildings the way we did three hundred years ago," said Safdie. "Although there have been drastic changes in the life of society—in its numbers and in its technology—our way of making cities, our reasons for making them, and our legislative tradition haven't changed.

"The tradition of individual owner-ship of land persists. Just as the thought of anybody buying up the sea or the rivers sounds grotesque, it should be obvious to everybody that land must be a public commodity. But we persist in a tradition which comes from a rural society where ownership of land was feasible and desirable, because only through ownership did you take the trouble to maintain, protect, and use the land."

If each family got an acre, the city could wind up three miles wide and four thousand miles long. Safdie dismissed that notion, and proposed instead a density of one to three hundred families per acre—which could make a city from ten to forty miles long and three miles wide.

Why so many families to the acre? Safdie's reasoning was plain: he wants urban environment together with open space; business facilities and recreation room; a variety of choices in shops and theatres, museums and restaurants. The ideal, he suggested, would be communities of about thirty thousand people—with the families in each community able to share the life of the twelve or fifteen million people in the city. As he wrote in his book: "The ideal environment would have the variety of Manhattan's amenities and the recreation space of the seacoast or the open spaces of New England as part of

daily experience, close enough so that you could enjoy both every day."

Safdie envisions great urban centers that would consist of Habitat-type living centers, perhaps eighty stories high, like membranes facing sun and sky, surmounting a base of five to seven stories containing commercial space, meeting space, and cultural facilities.

He suggested that within fifteen minutes' walking distance a family should find shopping facilities of at least 100,000 square feet, a mixture of cultural and recreational facilities, an elementary school, and employment opportunities. In a ten-minute drive one should be able to reach shopping facilities of at least 500,000 square feet, high schools, "a major park," and "major employment opportunities."

"In the city one should not have to move over great distances, but one requires mobility. It's built into an apartment building; pressing a button and riding up to the twentieth floor is something that we take for granted. The thought that we'd have to walk up twenty floors is incomprehensible. And yet the thought of having to walk blocks or wait ten minutes for a packed bus and then switch to an even more crowded one, or go underground and be packed like sardines, or drive—which is impossible in a city like New

"An Elaborate Gear System"

In the city of choice, mechanical transportation would be synchronized "like an elaborate gear system such as you might see in a watch." The sketch at right shows such a system, with trains slowing down at transfer zones in the city and coupling briefly with urban subways. All the city's intermeshed machinery of public transportation—from commuter trains to chair lifts to elevators to moving sidewalks—would work like a single "giant complex of geared wheels, all turning simultaneously at different speeds, and never stopping."

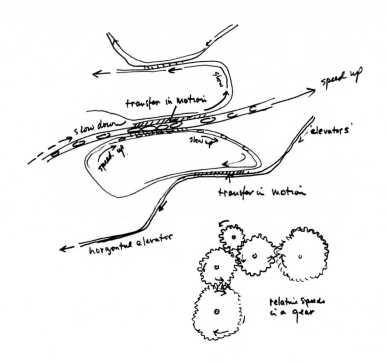

York—is comparable to living in a fifty-story building with the elevator removed.

"If you draw all the networks of movement in New York, vertically and horizontally, it's a very intricate three-dimensional network in which we move at random points. Unfortunately, we're not always going the same routes, because that could be easily solved."

Safdie maintained that systems of horizontal and vertical movement, allowing random movement without waiting in unpleasant surroundings, will be invented. "We're talking about synchronized, multidirectional, variable speed," he said. "It's like an elaborate gear system such as you might see in a watch, each gear moving at a different speed in a different place; at the points where they meet they're moving together, so that you can just flow from one wheel to the other, never stopping.

"It's less important for me to try to invent it than to define it, because its invention would be a process and not a single act, and once the problem is defined there might be many solutions."

He suggested that breaking up the city into independent, self-contained neighborhoods was no solution at all, and cited Brasília as an example of a theory that has proved fallacious in practice.

Safdie considers New York and Los

Angeles two poles of development: "In Los Angeles the structure of the city suggests very few random contacts between people, because the opportunity for that contact is not there unless you decide to go and see somebody. If you're moving on the freeway in your own car, the only way to have contact with anyone is to have an accident.

"New York is a place full of contact, but the social realities in New York have meant that violence, tensions, and a feeling of insecurity have made people withdraw. People say, 'You can't build Habitat in New York because you wouldn't be able to police it.' Or, 'You can't have all these open public spaces because people won't use them.' Or, 'You can't have parks because nobody goes into Central Park—it's not safe.'"

Safdie does not believe that even his kind of city would solve the problems of public safety. Indeed, he feels that these problems must first be corrected if the environment is to improve.

"The ideal of a city is a subtle thing," he said, "and it's more difficult to talk about it and define it than to discuss the advantages of efficient technology in building. When you get the United States government interested in housing, it's easier for them to rationalize spending money on getting new hard-

ware tried out or changing building codes or getting the unions to co-operate with new methods of production than it is to persuade them that the housing we have been building for the majority of the population has not provided for the way people might want to live.

"The businessman's parameters and ambitions are clear, and you can deal with them," he went on. "They can break you, but you know what they are. Usually his antagonism or objection to a proposal is based on the fact that he feels he might lose money, and he may be absolutely right. So all he's doing is testing the reality of your proposal, and you respect that. What he's telling you is that the system can't take what you propose, because people don't spend much on housing. Most of my time is spent on the gap between the ideals for housing and cities and the realities of space and densities and economics.

"But that's much less frustrating than dealing with the government official who has some authority, a planner or architect or engineer, who tells you that you can't pour concrete on 45-degree walls, and you know you've done it fifty times before."

To persuade officialdom and improve the lot of the governed, Safdie proposes an environmental bill of

rights. It would secure to the citizen, as a matter of right, minimal environmental standards of space and privacy and comfort.

"When you say in an environmental bill of rights that a family should be able to live without hearing the neighbors, very few politicians would tell you no," he suggested. "The next step would be that the Federal Housing Administration would have to change its standards of construction. So step number one is to define the problem, step number two is the process of changing things.

"I would begin with a bill of rights which applies to the house, then to the community, and eventually to the city. For example, a fundamental right in the city would be free movement, provided as a basic service. You don't pay to come up in an elevator—and you should have the same right in horizontal transport."

Aesthetics would not be an enumerated right. Safdie dislikes the very word. Time and again he has presented a building scheme, and then been asked: what about the aesthetics of the thing?

"Aesthetics has to do with the sense of identity and light and space and privacy and ability to undergo manipulation—it's the result of all that, and not a thing in itself," he said.

"I don't think it's possible to work in an office building for a year or two and then say, 'How beautiful it is, but I roast in summer and I freeze in winter, and somebody stares at me through a glass wall every time I sneeze, and I can't concentrate because it's too noisy.'

"It doesn't make sense to pass a great big mirror tower and say in a detached way that it's a beautiful environment, but it doesn't work. The separation between experience and observation which is true of most art today is an unhealthy split in the culture. We find ourselves calling a car beautiful though it's unstable on the road, and a raincoat lovely though it doesn't keep out the rain."

An increasing number of clients are prepared to believe that he is right, and thus assure him almost continual movement from one urban environment to another. In addition to the Habitat under construction in Puerto Rico, Safdie is working on other projects here and abroad, supervising them from his Montreal office and at the sites.

For Baltimore he is planning a new community—Coldspring—for about twelve thousand people on a 570-acre site. Near Ottawa he is designing a large recreational facility for executives. As consulting architect to the Squamish Indians of Vancouver, who are looking for investment opportunities in real estate, he is advising on development of 500 acres in the city center. Recently he submitted a preliminary scheme for New York's Battery Park City project.

Safdie commutes from Canada, his home since 1954, to his native Israel, where he is working on a variety of projects. For the Israeli government, Safdie has designed housing for a number of scattered sites, principally in Jerusalem. A new yeshiva built according to his plan is now rising opposite the Wailing Wall, on the site of an ear-

lier yeshiva destroyed in 1948. Safdie considers this his best building yet.

He has been commissioned to plan the entire block of buildings opposite the Wailing Wall—and to design the plaza in front of it. He wants to restore the whole area to its level in King Herod's time, which means digging down almost thirty feet. And, in a former no man's land between the Old and New cities, he is building a commercial area, with shops, offices, parks, and parking facilities. He would now like to try his hand at constructing a whole new city, for which he has already done considerable planning.

"You have to be a little crazy to start with," he said, "to propose things that are far from the norm. You doubt yourself all the time, at least I do. When the opposition is really strong, I begin to wonder if perhaps my proposals are slightly nutty. But then I read interviews with people living in Habitat, telling how their whole perception of nature has changed, and my optimism returns. There are 158 apartments in Habitat—and a waiting list of about two hundred families. I've convinced myself that *they* can't all be nutty."

It was clearly one of those better days—when radical change appeared possible, when problems and solutions seemed clear, and when a road beckoned the traveler around the Avalanches of Skepticism. Over the past eight years, Safdie's zeal has been infectious: when he pushes out toward a horizon of greater Delight, he is no longer the solitary pilgrim.

Israel Shenker, who writes on a variety of topics for The New York Times, *contributed an article on Noam Chomsky to the Spring, 1971, issue of* HORIZON.

BILLY WILDER'S
SOME LIKE IT HOT

Billy Wilder took the plot from a forgotten German script, hung it on a Chicago gangland massacre, coaxed a moving performance from a star who couldn't act, and brought off a masterpiece of farce

"Nobody's perfect." Possibly that is the most famous last line of any American film. Well, nobody, nothing, *is* perfect—perhaps. *Some Like It Hot,* the picture that closes with that line, is almost the exception to the rule. It may be somewhat ungrateful to call a very funny film a masterpiece of its kind; it sounds like an attempt to take it out of human circulation. Still, Billy Wilder has brought it on himself. What is worse, I have to insist that this unfailingly delightful farce is a triple milestone.

It is significant three ways in American film history. It is the best film (so far) by the last European director to flourish in this country. It is the best film of the last great sex star created by Hollywood. It is the last of the carefree American comedies that sprang up when sound came in, bloomed through the thirties, and had a revival after the Second World War.

Hollywood has seen two principal "waves" of European directors. The first group, including such men as Ernst Lubitsch and F. W. Murnau, were imported in the twenties by an American industry that was jealous of European artistic advances and worried about commercial competition. The second group were the political refugees of the thirties. No European director has made a career in America since the war. Wilder is one of the last fruits of a cer-

On the opposite page, director Billy Wilder demonstrates for Marilyn Monroe how she should walk down the platform during her entrance for Some Like It Hot, *filmed in 1959. Above, she carries out his instructions.*

tain kind of cultural cross-pollination.

He was born Samuel Wilder in Vienna in 1906 and was called Billy by his mother, who was mad for everything American. He worked as a journalist and in the late 1920's went to Berlin, at that time probably the most sophisticated city in the world. He broke into films as a writer, moved to

France when Hitler moved to Berlin, wrote and co-directed there for about a year, then went to Hollywood in 1934, where for four years he did very little. In 1938 he joined with the American writer Charles Brackett and collaborated on a number of screenplays, including Garbo's *Ninotchka.* In 1942 he directed his first American film, *The Major and the Minor,* from a Wilder-Brackett script, and launched a career that included *The Lost Weekend, A Foreign Affair,* and *Sunset Boulevard.*

Through these years Wilder was acquiring a reputation for a mordantly amusing tone, a view of human behavior derived from the old-Berlin wittiness of Ernst Lubitsch and the scathing naturalism of Erich von Stroheim. Wilder had worked for Lubitsch on *Ninotchka,* and Stroheim worked for *him* in *Five Graves to Cairo* (in which he played Rommel) and *Sunset Boulevard.* Aided by American collaborators, Wilder was making his own mixture of European and domestic influences, growing more and more skillful as he proceeded.

Another fusion lay ahead of him. Marilyn Monroe, hush-voiced, moist-lipped, all made of whipped cream, burst on the world in 1950, and, retrospectively at least, it seems inevitable that her wide-eyed sexiness would some day encounter Wilder's winking appreciation of it. In 1955 they worked together on *The Seven Year Itch,* made

Adrift in Prohibition Chicago, two musicians, Joe (Tony Curtis) and Jerry (Jack Lemmon), accidentally witness the Saint Valentine's Day massacre.

from a Broadway comedy. Then Wilder found a new collaborator, I. A. L. Diamond; and in 1959 the United States, in the persons of Diamond, Monroe, Jack Lemmon, and Tony Curtis, combined with Europe, in the persons of Wilder and a man named Thoeren, to create a farcical gem.

Who was Thoeren? Most reference books merely attribute the original idea of *Some Like It Hot* to a story by R. Thoeren and M. Logan. In response to an inquiry, Wilder wrote me recently that he had no idea who M. Logan was but that Robert Thoeren was an old chum from the Berlin days who had been a handsome actor, had co-au-

thored a German film called *Fanfaren der Liebe (Fanfares of Love)*, had come to Hollywood as a scriptwriter, where he had prospered, and had urged Wilder to remake his film. Wilder was otherwise involved, but after Thoeren died in the mid-fifties, an agent raised the matter again.

"We got a print of the German original and ran it. It was quite poor, a rather heavy-handed Bavarian *Charlie's Aunt*, replete with dirndls and lederhosen. And yet there was that platinum nugget: two male musicians latching onto an all-girl band. So the property was purchased. . . . and my collaborator I. A. L. Diamond and I started from scratch."

The time they chose was perfect for the piece: the height of the Prohibition era—remote enough to be slightly romantic, near enough for easy identification. The plot concerns Joe, a saxophone player, and Jerry, a bass fiddler, both young and broke, who accidentally witness the Saint Valentine's Day massacre of one gang by another in Chicago in 1929. The victorious gang chief, Spats Colombo, wants the witnesses killed, but they manage to escape. Penniless, frantic to flee Chicago, they dress as girls and grab two jobs they know about, with an all-girl band headed for a Florida hotel.

On the train they meet the luscious band vocalist, Sugar Kane, who hopes to catch a millionaire at the resort hotel. When they arrive, an aging playboy millionaire appears, named Osgood Fielding, but he falls for the disguised Jerry, now called Daphne. Meanwhile, Joe, disguised as Josephine, redisguises himself after working hours as a millionaire in order to woo Sugar. Things are progressing steadily toward just normal madness when suddenly Spats appears at the hotel for a gangland convention.

A rival gang chief has Spats killed at a banquet, a murder that Joe and Jerry

Berth rites: Safe on the train with the girls in the band, Josephine (alias Joe) and Daphne (Jerry) rehearse (1) with the luscious vocalist Sugar Kane (Marilyn Monroe). Jerry suffers (2) when Sugar visits his berth later for some girl-talk; hoping for privacy, he checks the lower berth (3) and briefly relishes an intimate drink with Sugar (4), only to have his tête-à-tête give way to a crowded free-for-all (5, 6).

1.

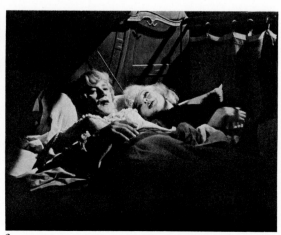

2.

3.

also accidentally witness. Now, doubly dangerous to the gangsters, they flee again. Sugar pursues Joe because she realizes, through a good-bye kiss, that her bandstand girl friend is really the "millionaire" she loves. Both of them, with Jerry, speed with Osgood out to his yacht. Osgood talks about wedding plans with Jerry, who is still in female dress, and dismisses Jerry's frantic objections. At last Jerry is forced to rip off his wig and say he can't marry Osgood because he's a man—to which the smiling, unswervable Osgood replies with the famous last line.

Like many good directors, Wilder began as a scriptwriter. Such a director knows that poor films can be made from good scripts but that good films cannot be made from poor scripts. This Wilder-Diamond script is a model of what farce should be.

The dialogue is not a collection of gags but a temperamental use of language: that is, vernacular is filtered through a chuckling temperament, diction is selected and arranged so that, while the characters speak always as themselves, the lines support and further the tone and action of the whole. Often a line gets a laugh, as when Jerry, after dancing until dawn with Osgood, says he has news for Joe, then tells him flatly: "I'm engaged." The laughs are pleasant when they come, but the triumph of the writing is that even when we don't laugh, the dialogue is funny.

In addition, there is a deft, knitted use of ideas. Themes are stated that are played back at odd angles. When the "girls" report for their jobs, the suspicious leader asks them their musical backgrounds, and they say they studied

Pursued by gangsters bent on rubbing them out, Joe and Jerry don women's clothing and wobble toward membership in a Florida-bound all-girl band.

at the Sheboygan Conservatory, which awes the others. Later, when Sugar is trying to impress Joe-as-millionaire, she tells *him* that she studied at Sheboygan. Early, when Joe cajoles a booking agent's secretary into lending him her car, it's a Hupmobile. Much later, as the millionaire, when he invents a traumatic love affair to impress Sugar, it is with the daughter of the vice-president of Hupmobile. These interwoven strands are a comic-dramatic bonus: the authors' humor employed as the characters' ingenuity.

Structurally, the script obeys and profits by two traditional formal injunctions for farce. First, it conforms

to Hebbel's all-inclusive dictum on the secret of dramatic style: "To present the necessary in the form of the accidental." Second, it begins with a ridiculous but engaging premise (Wilder's "nugget"), then builds on this improbable premise with rigid logic.

The one arguable moment in the logic of *Some Like It Hot* is the appearance of Spats at the very hotel where the band happens to be playing. It looks more necessary than accidental. Still, anyone who has heard an audience's response to the first sight of those spatted shoes in the hotel doorway knows that as soon as Spats appears, the audience realizes that they

Daphne (Jerry) tangos till dawn with an ardent admirer, millionaire Osgood Fielding (Joe E. Brown). To keep step with Osgood, he forsakes high heels.

Joe, whose change we will come to, none of them alters through the film, and almost none of them has, or is meant to have, depth. The exception is Sugar Kane, born Sugar Kovalchik, from Sandusky, Ohio. Marilyn Monroe.

The story of the making of this film is thickly laced with troubles—Wilder's troubles with the temperamental, unreliable, slow-learning Monroe. The reasons for her personality problems are not our business here; the result of the friction is. And that result is all the more astonishing because of the stormy off-screen story. The character as written and the performance that Wilder got from Monroe take the part beyond the jiggly-breasted sex doll of farce to a pathetic-comic portrait. The script was finished with her in mind: "We didn't think of Marilyn Monroe when we started plotting *Some Like It Hot*," says Wilder. "About half-way through we signed her and went back to fit her unique requirements . . ." Sugar is not just a cardboard blonde, she is a girl who has sexual power but no instinct for using it. She is the one, not the man, who gets "the fuzzy end of the

wanted him to appear, they wanted the increased complication.

Credibility in farce depends very much on this matter of what the audience wants to happen, without knowing they want it. The credibility is established with the fairly likely, based on references to life, then slides into the unlikely, based on references to the piece itself. Early in the film, when we see Joe wheedle the car out of the booking agent's secretary, we just about believe it could happen. Later, when Joe and Jerry decide to masquerade, the picture cuts to them wigged and in female dress. Where did this penniless

pair get the costumes so quickly? By now, we ourselves supply the wheedling that Joe did of some girl, and we do so both because of our experience of him and because we want the pair to be on that train with the band.

Farce, like melodrama, needs monochrome characters who will react predictably in given situations. *Some Like It Hot* has a well-blended spectrum of characters: the classic pair of youths, one aggressive and scheming, the other meek and wistful; the tough lady bandleader with the chromium smile; the nearsighted manager; the urbane, murdering Spats. With the exception of

Quick trip: Joe (alias Josephine) adopts yet another disguise. Aware that Sugar wants to meet a millionaire, Joe dresses the part, visits the beach while the girls play ball (1), causes Sugar to trip (2), and comes to her rescue (3). Enraged (4), Daphne drags Sugar to the hotel, hoping to catch Joe switching disguises (5). But Joe beats them home. Sugar finds Josephine in her tub, submerged in a cloud of bubbles (6) and leaves Daphne to discover the silver lining (7): one part girl, the rest sudsy "millionaire."

1.

2.

3.

4.

lollipop" in amorous encounters. She is the one who gets left, by the saxophone players who are her special weakness. It was diabolically insightful of Wilder and Diamond to build this role of a warmhearted loser for Monroe. It was good when the film first appeared; in the light of what happened to her finally, it becomes more touching, and her last-moment happiness in this picture is all the more exhilarating.

She couldn't really act. The sharp observer can see that she just about gets through some of her scenes without forgetting what she has been told to do. But she was a great screen personality. Wilder understood that, and how to "place" her personality on the screen. We often hear that there is no such thing as film acting because directors and editors control everything and can manufacture performances. We have only to see such a film as *La Grande Illusion* to know that, as fiat, this is false. But it *can* happen that way. A gifted director can use the medium to extract and construct a performance from a personality. Wilder does it here, superlatively.

Two other elements are used especially well. The first is a series of intracinematic references. When Joe poses as a millionaire, he employs a Cary Grant accent. When Spats arrives for the gangster convention, a young hood is idly flipping a coin in a doorway, and Spats says, "Where'd you pick up that stupid trick?" That coin trick was used in *Scarface*, twenty-seven years earlier, by George Raft, who plays Spats. At the gangster banquet, Spats picks up a grapefruit angrily, as if to shove it in a

Joe (posing as the girl-shy rich man) persuades Sugar Kane to give him lessons in love-making. Sugar is as eager to please as she is gullible.

henchman's face, something that James Cagney did to Mae Clarke in *The Public Enemy* in 1931. The subtlest reference, contained within the precincts of this film, is a scene, reminiscent of Restoration comedy, in which Joe, as the fake millionaire, pretends to be frigid and Sugar, anxious to hook him, kisses him and crawls all over him, trying to awaken his responses. The extra dimension of amusement comes from the fact that Sugar is not just a voluptuous girl, she is the girl who at that moment was probably the most-desired female on earth, and for a long time she cannot light any fire, apparently, in Joe.

The particular grace of these references is that they are inessential but enriching. If you don't understand them, you are not left out. If you do understand them, you sense how the history of film is being used in irreverent affection.

Second, there is Wilder's use of music. This is, quite literally, a musical comedy. When Sugar makes her first appearance, walking down the train platform like "Jello on springs," a muted trumpet comments just as it used to do when a stripper walked down the runway in burlesque. When the bus drives up to the gorgeous old Victorian hotel with the band, a girls'

chorus sings "Down Among the Sheltering Palms"; when the girls splash in for their first swim, the same chorus sings "By the Beautiful Sea." Both times, the songs blend with the sun and that wonderful hotel to keep our spirit both high and nostalgic.

But the best use of music is in Sugar's three songs. None is allowed to be just a static "number." On the train, when the girls rehearse "Runnin' Wild," Sugar drops a flask hidden in her stocking. Drinking is forbidden by the leader, and she is about to be fired. But Jerry pretends the flask is his, so the song becomes a chance to establish rapport. On the hotel bandstand, when Sugar sings "I Wanna Be Loved by You," Joe uses the last portion as a cover to switch cards on a big basket of flowers sent by Osgood. Near the end, after Sugar's "millionaire" has phoned to say he is leaving suddenly, she sings "I'm Through with Love," again on the bandstand, and Joe, the fake millionaire, realizes how she feels and how *he* feels.

Joe is Tony Curtis, who has sometimes done well in other films but has never done better than here. He charges the role to the brim with comic energy; his timing is crisp; and his change of heart at the end, from exploiter to lover, is affectingly underplayed. Jack Lemmon is Jerry, and as always in his best comic performances, he combines clean vocal attack and nicely shaded readings with a feeling for silent-comedy profile. The moment on the beach when Jerry, in a girl's bathing suit, runs past his pal Joe posing as a millionaire and recognizes Joe only after he has passed, stopping with one foot raised—that moment is one of the best delayed "takes" since Buster Keaton.

Occasionally the word "transvestite" is applied to *Some Like It Hot* in a clinical sense, as if the film were an unwitting glimpse into psychosexual murk. Literally, the term "transvestite" is accurate; psychically, it applies about as much as it does to *Der Rosenkavalier* because Octavian is played by a woman. Wilder shot the film in black and white

"I'm a man," Jerry shouts at the enamored Osgood, above, but the news fails to register. Opposite, singing "I'm Through with Love," in the film's most moving scene, Sugar mourns the disappearance of her millionaire. Like the star who played her, Sugar is victimized by her own warm heart, beauty, and —oddly enough for a sex queen—innocence.

(against Monroe's wishes) because he thought that in color the two male leads would be accused of transvestism if their make-up was light or of vulgarism if it was heavy. The masquerade comedy comes, not from swishing about, but from the very maleness of two young men in a harem situation and unable to do anything about it. The upper-berth party, with Jerry in nightdress visited by a horde of pretty girls in nightdresses, is a scene of hilarious torture. Sometimes the viewer of sex comedy needs a little less glib psychology and a little more innocence.

It would be foolish to burden *Some Like It Hot* with undue praise. I am interested in due praise. The beauty—no less a word will do—of a fine farce like this has little to do with the elements of high comedy: character dissection, moral reproof, social comment. There is no valid social comment in this picture: the gang wars, Sugar's millionaire-hunting, Osgood's profligate philandering, are used only as props. Wilder and Diamond were interested not in indicting American mores but in utilizing them. Their purpose was to make us laugh.

Watching their picture is like watching good trapezists. They, too, start from a ridiculous premise: what sane person would hang from bars in midair? Once there, they proceed with absolute logic. Farce gives us the thrill of danger (when Joe forgets to take off his

bandstand earrings, racing to a date as the millionaire) and the thrill of split-second neatness (when he whisks them off just in time). Basically, that is the greatest joke of all: absolute order has been imposed on the chaos of life. Farce, as an artistic form, is identical with that order. We know that life, on either side of these two hours, is chaotic. There is pleasure here in seeing how neatly things fit together for people we like.

Possibly, to come finally to the third significance of *Some Like It Hot*, that is why it is the last really good farce produced in this country to date. There have been new imitations of old farces, there have been new attempts, all inferior; they lack any real commitment to the sheer fun of design, to the ideal of a finely turned comic machine.

Also, the great *farceurs* believed very strongly in physical movement: running, sliding, hurtling, wheeling, bicycling, jumping, climbing, and falling (Monroe is tripped for a headlong fall). The latter-day screwball comedies, which is Hollywood jargon for farce, lack real conviction in the moving body as a source of wonders.

I regret ending on a serious note, but many viewings of *Some Like It Hot* have convinced me that it belongs in the line of the best elegantly busy farces of the last century, the line of Labiche and Feydeau and Pinero. Those farces exist in a kind of limbo: they can be revived well or ill. The script of a film is inseparably wedded to its performance, whatever its quality may be; and *Some Like It Hot* is happily married to its fine performance forever. This film will make people laugh as long as future societies bear any perceptible relation to our own; and will make people laugh the second, third, or sixth time they see it. If that isn't immortality, it's close enough. Nobody's perfect.

Some Like It Hot can be rented in 16 mm. form from United Artists 16, 729 Seventh Avenue, New York, New York 10019. The screenplay has, alas, not yet been published.

Lordly Pleasures

Secure in their wealth, confident of their position, indulged by their countrymen, the aristocrats of eighteenth-century England did their own thing, and in doing it, invented our ideals of civilized living

They were the children of time: the Rolles of Devon, the Cholmondeleys of Cheshire, the Greys and Hastings of Leicestershire, the Knatchbulls of Kent, the Walpoles and Townshends of Norfolk. The lands upon which they lived had been theirs since the Middle Ages or earlier. Some, like the Okehovers of Okehover, went straight back, son to father, beyond the Norman Conquest to Saxon times.

Their own memorials littered their landscapes, their churches, and their houses: bits of castles, relics of ancient homes, oaks planted by ancestors almost lost in antiquity, recalled that the past was theirs; in church, effigies in marble or etched in brass gave them their long continuance; in their halls and dining rooms the portraits of their more recent dead enfolded them in the same sense of security in time. Here they had always lived and ruled, marrying into families like their own, so that

across the English lands by 1750 there was a network of aristocrats as closely knit to their lands as the roots of their forests were.

They did quarrel and fight with neighbors, sometimes pursuing their feuds over the centuries; some families rose, some fell, but most survived, like the great ancient oaks of their parks. Such antiquity, such social security, bred confidence, not necessarily confidence in oneself, for there were plenty of noblemen and gentlemen capable of self-doubt, but social confidence, not only in their present status but also in its continuing future. What had so long endured was unlikely to come to an abrupt end. Given reasonable luck and healthy sons, given reasonable prudence in the management of their estates, they could be sure that where they lived, so would their descendants for all foreseeable time. Hence they could plan the future—remove hills, dig lakes, divert rivers and roads, plant

forests, not for themselves (indeed, they might never see the forests), but for their children and their children's children. What did it matter if a new mansion might absorb the income of a lifetime, when so many more lifetimes were to follow!

For the first time they had—as a class—money in abundance. Of course, there had been rich noblemen before the eighteenth century who had poured money into the delights of life, who had lived in extravagant and costly ostentation. One has only to think of the Elizabethan aristocracy with its finery, its castles, and its parade of servants

With the correct eighteenth-century air of studied nonchalance, Thomas Coltman, opposite, of Lincolnshire, prepares to go riding with his wife. The portrait, by Joseph Wright, was done around 1772. At the time, wealthy gentlemen like Coltman, titled or not, had more scope for their talents and whims than perhaps any other privileged class in history.

and retainers. But in Tudor days aristocrats were fewer, and their ostentation was an expression of pride, like a potlatch among the Kwakiutl Indians, who burned their blankets and smashed their sacred coppers to show how magnificent it was to do so. Frequently the Tudor aristocracy was desperately in debt.

But in the eighteenth century, due to the profits of improved agriculture, the expanding worldwide commerce of England, and the growing security of government finances, a large class of men—gentry as well as aristocrats—felt secure in their wealth as never before. And there was an even more subtle factor at work: the beginning of what we would now call consumer capitalism. It seemed good to spend—on trinkets and clothes, on houses and gardens, on sports and pastimes, on food and drink and all that delighted the eye,

stirred the mind, or soothed the heart. And thus, with increasing affluence and a growing pressure to spend, the nobility and gentry of eighteenth-century England created a style of life that was elegant, self-indulgent, worldly, and immensely cultivated in the best sense of that abused word. Some of their pleasures were gross, many eccentric; but as a class their pleasures adorned their world and left posterity with a remarkable heritage.

Perhaps their best legacy was their

greatest passion—building and planting. Although they took pride in tracing their ancestors back to the Conquest or even, arrogantly, to the Romans, and boasted of their lineage in the heraldic embellishments that they engraved or painted or wove on all they possessed, they had little use for the taste of their ancestors. They ruthlessly demolished the rambling Tudor and Stuart manor houses or swallowed them up in the new Palladian palaces and villas that became the hallmark of aristocratic good taste.

Even before the Earl of Burlington, who in 1715 began to promote Palladio's designs in England, the rage for building had taken hold. Sir John Vanbrugh had created several really enormous houses—the vast palace of Blenheim, a baroque monument fit for a sovereign prince; the gigantic Castle Howard with its extravagantly long façade; and Sea-

74

John Zoffany's portrait of the daughters of the third Earl of Bute

ton Delaval in the wilds of Northumberland. Burlington and his painter-decorator henchman, William Kent, turned this growing appetite for building into a mania. Gentlemen became architects and architects became gentlemen. As with all fads, it had its moments of lunacy: one lady at court persuaded Kent to design her a dress embroidered with the five orders of columns.

Enthusiasm combined with considerable architectural knowledge added greatly to the pleasures of life. The young nobleman on tour visited Vicenza, Padua, Venice, and then ordered his hired painter to sketch the villas, so that the ancestral house in Yorkshire or Lancashire might be accordingly embellished. To contemporaries in England the first Neo-Renaissance houses were bewildering. The façade of Burlington's house in Piccadilly staggered Lon-

doners; the Kentish folk had seen nothing like the huge dome at Mereworth Castle, which was a copy of Palladio's rotunda outside Vicenza. Now, however, these Palladian houses look as natural to the English countryside as the Tudor manor houses that survive. These men were building villas not for themselves but for eternity. Private pleasure was enhanced by a sense of family duty. Within a mere thirty years, from 1710 to 1740, more than one hundred and forty great country

Commanding a view of bucolic "nature" artfully arranged, Shugborough, county seat of Thomas Anson, looked daringly neoclassical in 1769, when this painting was done. Dotting the park are decorative structures known as follies, designed to enliven the view.

houses were either built or remodeled.

The building craze did more: it helped root the English country gentleman even more firmly into his estates. New buildings created new problems, for a house requires a setting just as a picture needs a frame. A few parterres on the French or Dutch model, a canal with formal buildings, or a few vistas cutting each other at right angles were previously all that was deemed necessary. The grander the house, the grander the parterre, the more ornate the canal, the more numerous and geometric the vistas; however, ambition was kept within restrained and formal limits.

Zoffany's companion portrait of the Earl's three sons at play

75

The eighteenth-century country gentleman, however, put few limits to his pleasures, as we shall see, and he took over not merely the acres surrounding his home but the whole landscape as far as the eye could see. If need be, he razed villages that disturbed the view.

The first Earl Bathurst, a tree fancier, created about his house at Cirencester a forest through which he carved out glades and serpentine walks, dotting them with whimsical buildings that had even more whimsical names—Alfred's Hall, Pope's Seat, The Horseguards, Ivy Lodge, and the Silvan Bower. In the long summer evenings Lord Bathurst took his guests to Alfred's Hall where they could dine alfresco and drink their claret in the cool evening shade. But a wood decorated with follies, as they were called, was not enough. Whatever the cost, a gentleman's landscape must have water—so Bathurst dug out a lake—not a formal canal, but a lake that seemed as natural as if God himself had placed it there. Still the landscape did not look finished: a hill seemed to spoil a diagonal view, so Bathurst had it leveled. Once leveled, it left a gap so vast that the prospect needed something to catch the eye. He toyed with a pyramid, played with the idea of an obelisk, and finally decided on a huge Doric column topped with a more than life-sized statue of Queen Anne.

Lord Bathurst lived to be ninety-one and never stopped adorning his forest: running into debt, selling estates, buying others, pouring out money on statues, columns, follies, and whimsies. Until the month he died, he rode about his park for two or three hours in all weather and refreshed himself every evening by downing a bottle of claret or Madeira. Self-indulgent, wanton, extravagant, obsessed, one might say, but two hundred years later Lord Bathurst's delights still charm the eye and improve on nature. He created a landscape that now seems as natural as the Cotswold Hills, but is entirely the work of a man who knew how to

CHARLES JAMES FOX

Son of a wealthy baron and grandson of a duke, Charles James Fox was born into the inner circle of privilege and made the most of it. By the age of twenty-five he was £140,000 in debt, an addict of the gaming tables, corpulent with good food and high living, and one of the leading politicians in the country. Good-tempered, buoyant, and magnanimous, Fox never fretted about the consequences of his acts. He rose to deliver his speeches with no further preparation than twenty hours spent playing hazard. He fell in love with a humbly born woman and made her his wife. He decided that George III was a tyrant and made the king his implacable political enemy. In good times and bad, Fox always followed his own bent with the greatest aplomb and good cheer. "To the day of his death," David Cecil observed, "I do not suppose he ever did anything he did not like."

please himself as well as posterity.

Bathurst was a pioneer, pointing the way for Capability Brown, the great landscape gardener of eighteenth-century England who laid out such masterpieces as Chatsworth, one of the noblest parks in England. Brown also created the two vast lakes at Blenheim, providing an appropriate setting for Vanbrugh's palace. Indeed, Brown's alterations to the park cost the Duke of Marlborough £30,000 (about $1,-500,000 in modern money—a high price for the pleasure of picnicking on the water or angling for a pike). Today, strolling along the terraces of many English country houses, with their vistas of woods and meadows and the reflected light of their distant lakes, one is moved to praise the beauties of nature, except that, indeed, all is manmade. As far as the eye can see, it is all contrived. Often it has come to full maturity only centuries after it was conceived: the villagers of Church Langton complained bitterly that their parson, William Hanbury, was so crazed with his plantations that he totally neglected his clerical duties; his woods and avenues are now the village's greatest beauty.

Of course, the insides of their houses attracted some noblemen as much as the landscapes in which they were set. If pictures and statues took their fancy, then, like Charles Towneley, they filled their houses with them; if books, then, like Edward Harley, they accumulated immense libraries. Inheriting a splendid collection from his father, Robert Harley, the great Tory statesman of Queen Anne's reign, Edward added to it with such zest that he brought himself to the edge of bankruptcy. By the time of his death he possessed 50,000 printed books, 350,000 pamphlets, 41,000 prints, and 8,000 volumes of priceless manuscripts that became a foundation of the British Museum's collection. He hungered for books as some men hunger for drink or women.

The aristocrat's instinctive belief that he was superior to the rest of humankind, combined with a strong dose of inbreeding, produced, as one might expect, a wonderful forcing ground for human eccentricity. After all, who was going to say no? Certainly not the easygoing, permissive, amused society of Georgian England.

No one was more bent on pleasure than George Walpole, Earl of Orford, the grandson of Sir Robert Walpole, once prime minister. Orford inherited the great house of Houghton, containing the finest collections of old masters in England. The world of poli-

Making Life Sweet

At the outset of the eighteenth century the life of the English country gentry was far from easy and relaxed. Their stiff formality and their half-feudal punctilio was a common butt of humor for town wits and coxcombs. By the second half of the century, however, Addison's urbane reminder that "Nothing is so modish as an agreeable Negligence" was rapidly permeating the life of the squire, who now began combining the gaiety and refinement of the town with the spacious comforts of the manorial estate. To mirror this new, urbane way of life, a highly specialized form of painting came into fashion. This was the Conversation Piece, which portrayed groups of real people enjoying a pleasant moment within their own fine homes or outdoors on their own handsome estates, as in Gainsborough's painting, above, of the Gravenor family, done around 1748. To those who commissioned one, perhaps from John Zoffany, the acknowledged master of the genre, the conversation piece provided a permanent testimonial to their success in the chief endeavor of the age: making life as sweet as possible. How well lordly England succeeded is amply, indeed poignantly, attested by the conversation pieces shown on these pages.

The Duke and Duchess of Atholl and their seven eldest children go fishing on the ducal estate while a pet marmoset looks on. As if epitomizing the gentry

blending of town and country, Zoffany painted the figures in London while another artist did the background at Blair Castle, the Duke's Scottish seat.

Lord Willoughby de Broke, above, appears in a typical Zoffany conversation piece, gently admonishing his daughter in the breakfast room at Compton Verney. The silver tea urn, designed by one of the celebrated Adam brothers, is still in the family's possession. Below, the Anglo-Irish gentry of Kildare watch Lord Aldborough, mounted on his favorite horse, Pomposa (left), reviewing his troops on the well-tended turf of Belan Park, his county seat.

tics or of fashion awaited him—in vain. He preferred horses, greyhounds, boats, and Mrs. Patty Turk. Mrs. Turk, whom all his friends admired, had been a strikingly beautiful maid at Houghton. Becoming his mistress, she stayed with him until she died, and he remained totally devoted to her. This lifelong passion was undoubtedly responsible for his withdrawal from aristocratic society into the world of jockeys, breeders, and boatmen—a world in which Patty could act as hostess.

Usually he lived on a small property, Eriswell, near to both Newmarket and the Fens. Indeed, he styled himself Admiral of the Fens and created a small fleet of boats—bumboats, admiral's barges, and fast yachts. With Mrs. Turk and his friends aboard, he would sail down the winding waterways to one of the greatest lakes in England, Whittlesea Mere, now long since drained. Bridges that impeded his progress were summarily removed. Once on the lake, Orford entertained Lord Sandwich, the First Lord of the Admiralty, who lived nearby at Hinchingbrooke. To the background of music over the water, they drank, feasted, fished, and raced in their sailboats. The country folk came from miles around to watch these aristocratic antics. The fiesta and regatta over, Orford sailed his stately fleet to Peterborough to dine with the bishop, whose pleasures ran to the table; he provided exquisite food and an exceptionally fine and delectable burgundy. Mrs. Turk was not invited.

Orford was self-indulgent and arrogant, and yet what a pleasure it must have been to hear the music floating over the water and watch the reflections of the gilded barges against the background of wide fenland skies. After all, what Orford and Sandwich were among the first to do is now done by tens of thousands, sailing not in great barges surely, but in tiny boats; and even though the English no longer have Whittlesea Mere, they still throng the narrow rivers. As in so many ways, the aristocracy pointed the way to pleasure for later multitudes.

THE DUCHESS OF DEVONSHIRE

For Georgiana, Duchess of Devonshire, life was a perpetual succession of enthusiasms. Taking up the fad for science, she built a laboratory at her house to conduct chemical experiments. Taking up the craze for Rousseau and Nature, she dispensed with a wet nurse and suckled her own children, at least one of whom was illegitimate. Taking up the craze for gambling, she wound up owing one million pounds. Yet her ruinous debts, her legions of admirers, and her bubbling, eccentric enthusiasms never outraged fashionable society. Georgiana was, in fact, society's queen as well as its greatest delight. When she died in 1806, the Prince of Wales was heard to say: "We have lost the best-bred woman in England."

Orford loved boats, and Mrs. Turk, and horses, but he adored dogs and coursing more. In 1776 he set up the Swaffham Coursing Club, which convened with the extravagant ceremony that Orford required. He maintained a huge and expensive kennel and experimented widely in crossbreeding, matching bulldogs with greyhounds. He invented a sport—coursing a hare with greyhounds and whippets—that was to spread not only across England but into all classes as well. Nowadays it is the favorite sport of the grim mining towns of Yorkshire and Durham. Orford had less luck, however, with his falconers' society, The Confederate Hawks of Great Britain, although he spent as much money on hawks as he did on boats or dogs or horses, importing Dutch falconers, whom he rightly

thought to be superior to the English.

Like thistledown, Orford's passion for outdoor pleasures blew here and there, and sometimes he lost his wits entirely. No one in Norfolk could be sure when he might furiously concentrate all his energies on some new delight. As Lord Lieutenant of Norfolk during the wars with France, he ordered all villages and suburbs of Norwich to be razed should the enemy land, and threw himself into drilling the militia and outfitting them in a weird costume of long, loose white trousers and red smocks.

The common people of East Anglia loved him and thronged to his funeral, and a last glimpse we have of him in old age is in Parson Woodforde's diary: "Mounted on a stump of a pye-balled pony (as uniformly broad as he was long), in a full suit of black, without either great-coat or gloves, his hands and face crimsoned with cold, and in a fierce cocked hat facing every wind that blew; and while his gamekeepers were shrinking from the sand-gathering blasts of Norfolk, on he rode, like old Lear, regardless of the elements." Lear-like he might look in old age, but Orford had lived a life dedicated entirely to pleasure, regardless of the consequences. He sold off his grandfather's collection of pictures to Catherine of Russia. And he gave away the great flight of stairs from his grandfather's house. Still the debts piled up as he raced, coursed, dressed up his militia, and dallied with Patty. Like many of the aristocrats of his time, he insisted on living life on his own terms, no matter how odd they might seem to the rest of the world.

Most noblemen were more temperate and less extravagant, but they still put pleasure first. They designed their lives to expel boredom: in winter they hunted and shot; in summer they raced their horses and flocked to the theatres of their county towns (which they had helped build) to see a good London touring company playing the latest Sheridan, Goldsmith, or Foote. If rich enough and addicted to the theatre, then, naturally, like the Duke of Marlborough, they built their own. By 1800 more than a dozen large country houses were producing plays. Lord Barrymore had a theatre at each of his three houses, including his town house in Savile Row. In addition, they danced and gambled, either at home or in the classically proportioned assembly rooms of their county towns. Sometimes they went off to London or to Bath or to Tunbridge Wells for more urban pleasures; often they made long sightseeing tours to discover how other noblemen were building and planting. From time to time, they had to attend to the business of their estates, but it was rarely urgent, and life for many of them flowed as smoothly as the Thames. For the rich this was not an age of anxiety.

They were particularly good at entertaining each other, and country life became an endless round of dancing, music making among themselves, or playing charades; the weather benign, they would in the summertime take their meals alfresco on the lake or in the woods; in the winter months they skated or drove through their landscaped parks in beautifully ornamented sleighs.

Aristocratic society was permissive —not all of it, of course, but most of it—and so they pursued Venus as ardently as they did Bacchus or Diana. Love in all its forms amused them: they gossiped endlessly and lightheartedly about the adulterers, the lesbians, the homosexuals, or those aristocrats who hungered for the callused hands of working-class women. Hardly anything shocked them except an outrageous misalliance, and even that was forgivable for a man, though certainly not for a woman.

They knew how to avoid boredom. If country pleasures palled, they took themselves off to London for the early summer and the late fall, bent on more extravagance, such as dressing up for the formal balls to celebrate a royal birthday. Decked in their finery, they filled the boxes at the theatre and the opera, ogling and being ogled. Better still were the masquerades at Vauxhall

LORD ROKEBY

While other aristocrats indulged their whims in society, Matthew, Lord Rokeby, with equal self-assurance, chose to live the life of a hermit —on his own ample estate. Lord Rokeby believed passionately in Nature, the natural life, and prolonged submersion in water. To this purpose, he built a bathhouse in a wild grove on his land, and there he would soak his gnomelike figure for long hours each day, keeping a piece of meat by his elbow for ready consumption. His friends were the birds in his wood. His chief activity, it is said, was meditating on the Liberty of Man, and his chief delight as a man of property was letting his estate run to seed out of repugnance for all forms of artificiality.

and Ranelagh, where in disguise they could flirt and make assignations. They shopped as never before—these were the early days of Bond Street, with the latest fashions discreetly displayed through the new invention of the bay window. Wrought silver and plate, jewels and gold boxes, had never been so abundant or so eagerly sought. Josiah Wedgwood invited them to his warehouse to see his new wares laid out on glittering tables. Young men dressed with a care that their ancestors would have thought frivolous and a discretion that they would have thought odd. The cut of a coat, the fit of a boot, the fall of a cravat, were judged to a nicety and argued about endlessly.

Sometimes—as with the macaronis— the young bloods would burst out in peacock-like extravagances; but mostly Beau Brummell's austere concept of elegance prevailed.

Wherever they went, they gambled. It was the national mania, but the nobility led the way. Their great passion was horse racing, and they organized the Jockey Club, formalized the rules of racing, and set up an elaborate racing calendar so that great races never conflicted in date. And, of course, they established the racing classics—the Derby was named after the Earl of Derby, an obsessed racing man, and the St. Leger at Doncaster was named after his northern counterpart, Colonel St. Leger.

But horses assuaged only a part of their passion for gambling: in London the young noblemen took over coffeehouses—White's, Almack's, Crockford's—and turned them into private clubs whose main business was gambling at cards. Charles James Fox, the distinguished Whig politician and hero of the Westminster public, gambled away two fortunes at Brooks's before he reached middle age—indeed, before he was sixteen, he and his elder brother had got through £16,000 apiece in three days. The Earl of Sandwich found it impossible to drag himself away from the faro tables even for supper, so he dined there on two slices of bread stuffed with meat. Women gambled as passionately as men. Georgiana, Duchess of Devonshire—beautiful, elegant, and wanton—had no more self-control at cards than she had at love. She ruined herself beyond repair by her extravagant bets.

Cards and horses were major addictives, but so were prize fighting, cockfighting, and above all, cricket. Cricket developed its elaborate rules in the eighteenth century and became popular because it provided such a rich and complex situation for gambling. One could gamble not only on the result but also on an almost infinite number of chances within the game. If the ladies and gentlemen grew bored with the usu-

What Gentlemen Did

Eighteenth-century English gentlemen belonged to a leisured class, but their leisure was fiercely active. They took part in politics, in farming, in governing. They helped design their own homes and landscape their own estates. They were social leaders of their districts and patrons of its revels. Above all, the English country gentleman was an ardent sportsman. He fished his own streams, shot over his own land, chased deer and fox the length and breadth of the county. In their pursuit of energetic activity the eighteenth-century aristocracy took over the game of cricket, which had long been played on village greens such as the one depicted above, on the Isle of Wight. Supplying cricket with formal rules in 1744, lordly England turned an ancient rustic amusement into a fashionable game. Yet no gentleman had to be a bluff, hearty sportsman or, indeed, anything in particular. What is truly striking about the eighteenth century was its extraordinary openness. One gentleman might be a sportsman, another might well be a fop. One gentleman bred horses and hounds, another organized musicales and private theatricals. Whatever a gentleman did was what a gentleman was licensed to do. Possibly the only thing that was denied to the privileged class was the right to make money in "trade."

Under the knowing eye of the Duke of Richmond, jockeys exercise three of his sleek race horses while the Duchess and her sister

watch. The painting is by George Stubbs, who shared with Richmond and other aristocratic patrons a veritable mania for horses.

Transportation becomes an amusement: A couple take a ride in a phaeton, the light, open carriage much favored by the modish at the times Stubbs did this painting, in 1787. Below, members of the Cork Harbour Water Club, oldest of all yacht clubs, race for the Admiral's Cup in 1738.

al round of horses, cards, and games, they could and did gamble on anything. The few betting books that survive from the eighteenth century betray better than any other source the feckless abandon of young aristocrats who might bet on the fertility of a duchess, or a raindrop running down a pane of glass, or, perhaps most startling of all, whether, before the year was out, Lord Cholmondeley would copulate a thousand feet above London in one of the new balloons.

But gambling was not all extravagance and loss. In the 1780's the young bloods developed a passion for racing each other in their carriages from London to Brighton. Like our racing motorists, they and their carriage builders poured ingenuity and money into creating flimsy but extremely fast phaetons, which they drove with exceptional speed and skill. With Tommy Onslow, who once won twenty-five guineas from the Prince Regent by driving his phaeton and four at a gallop through two narrow gateways twenty-five times without touching them, Sir John and Lady Lade were aces at this sport. She swore like a fishwife, and in fact Sir John first made her acquaintance in a brothel on one of those rare occasions when he left his stables. Bankrupted by his passion for gambling, he finished his life happily enough as a coachman on the London-Brighton run, which he had done much to improve. The racing phaeton, like the racing motorcar, brought great technical improvement both to vehicles and to roads.

There were less attractive lordly pleasures. Arrogance and pride carried to the point of insanity, combined with adolescent boredom, produced outbursts of violence. Duels over trifling insults studded the century with corpses, but worse still were the cruel practical jokes and downright terrorism that the rich often practiced on innocent members of the lower classes. Rape, and other abuses, could be commited against servant girls and working women with near immunity. Some aggressive young noblemen found it practical-

SIR JOHN LADE

Sir John Lade enjoyed driving fast coaches, racing fast coaches, and betting on everything. He cared for very little else. The orphaned son of a wealthy baronet, he was so brainless a wastrel that Dr. Johnson told him to remain a bachelor: "I would advise no man to marry who is not likely to propagate understanding." Marry, however, Sir John did—a daredevil named Letty, the former mistress of both a criminal and a duke. At raffish, dissolute Brighton, the Lades capered in the limelight as boon companions of the Prince Regent, who shared their taste for racing, betting, and careening through narrow streets in a six-in-hand. Every inch a "sporting man," Sir John lived to a ripe old age, neither propagating understanding nor gaining any. Lade, wrote a wit of the time, will "always be—a lad!"

ly impossible to bridle their appetites.

There were, nevertheless, aristocrats whose natural bent was for the more gracious and rewarding pleasures of life. There were bookish peers, scientific peers, political peers, and even radical peers—essentially amateurs doing what they did because it both fulfilled and pleased them. Charles, third Earl Stanhope, was as much obsessed with science and radical politics as Lord Barrymore was with gambling and theatricals. Even as a boy he had shown remarkable skill not only in mathematics but also in mechanical contrivance. One of his most spectacular triumphs was to fireproof floors

and walls. To show off his invention, he assembled Lord Chatham, the Lord Mayor of London, and the president of the Royal Society and served them ice cream "while the most intense fire that could be made was raging in the room directly under it, and separated from it only by a common wooden floor." Later, his own house was saved from a disastrous fire because he had used his methods, which, indeed, remained the preferred means of fireproofing for the next hundred and fifty years.

He also invented the first calculating machine that could multiply and divide and was among the first to attempt to adapt Boulton and Watt's steam engine to the propulsion of ships. He added several modifications that helped make the adaptation possible. He was probably the first to devise stabilizers for ships, and when his friend Robert Fulton invented the explosive sea mine, Stanhope countered by devising the paravane, which could defuse mines. Turning to printing, he improved the stereotype plate and a press, named after himself, upon which *The Times* of London was printed for a generation.

Of course, he loftily refused to derive any pecuniary advantages from these inventions, which he insisted must be free for all to use. He never stopped inventing: new methods of burning lime, a paste for healing injured trees, a pocket magnifier that remained in use for a century. Altogether he spent well over £30,000 on indulging his delight in invention—no more than his fellow aristocrats might waste on girls or cards or horses.

Stanhope combined this love for practical inventions with a passion for radical politics. He denounced with repeated ferocity the repressive measures of his kinsman William Pitt. He approved of the American Revolution and welcomed the French Revolution with joy. He removed the earl's coronets that had graced his gateways and took to addressing—much to their astonishment—the gentlemen of Kent as "citizens" and signing himself "Citizen

Stanhope." To celebrate Pitt's failure to secure the conviction of a secretary on charges of "treasonable practices," Stanhope gave a ball for over four hundred people that lasted through the night. Naturally he was a passionate supporter of the reform of Parliament and the abolition of the slave trade; and so extreme were his views that he found himself in a minority of one in the House of Lords, from which he then seceded. The London radicals immediately struck a medal in his honor. When he returned to the House of Lords five years later, in 1800, he was still unsuccessful in his demands for peace with France, obtaining only one supporter. But serenely arrogant in his own convictions, Stanhope pursued science and radical politics until the end of his life. Not surprisingly, perhaps, he was a cold husband and an eccentric father, but in this he was certainly not alone among the peerage.

Proud and self-indulgent, careless of the present because they were so confident of the future, these aristocrats not only explored the world of pleasure but developed patterns of living so appealing that what they alone enjoyed in their own day is now available to all. The fenland rivers that Lord Orford and Lord Sandwich once adorned with their elegant regatta are now alive with small boats. Horse-racing rules developed in the eighteenth century by the Derbys, Rutlands, Godolphins, Seftons, and St. Legers were first adopted by France and America, then finally by the world. And the English aristocracy and gentry were the first to bring the sophistications of city life to their country houses and to combine the pleasures of country life with urbanity. After shooting in the wild Derbyshire hills, they returned to Chatsworth, replete with old masters and exquisite French furniture, to dine and drink as well as Louis XV did. In a house that could accommodate a hundred guests and their servants, no one could be bored with the isolation of rural life. The men would shoot and fish, and sometimes so would the women. All would dance, gossip, and flirt. In these spacious country houses it was also easy to drift away and read or to wander in the artlessly artful landscape. The weekend visit—that splendid institution of the eighteenth-century rich —took form later at a simpler level: a group of mutual friends with common interests entertaining each other, but reposefully.

The eighteenth century also brought into being many towns designed for leisure—Bath, Tunbridge Wells, Matlock, Scarborough—where the rich indulged themselves and then eased the consequences by taking the purging waters that these spas provided. From such elegant beginnings sprang the huge leisure centers of today.

But their most important legacy, perhaps, was what they prized most— their freedom to be themselves. Few societies until modern times have given such freedom to individuals. The old feudal concepts of the role of aristocracy had broken down in the revolutionary years of seventeenth-century England, and by the time aristocracy re-established its social status, it had freed itself from traditional patterns of behavior. True, it still possessed power, still regarded itself as the natural companion of royalty, still retained a patriarchal attitude to the tenants of its estates, but there was no fixed image of itself. Individualism—the hallmark of bourgeois society—combined with aristocratic confidence, allowed every variety of human temperament to flourish untrammeled. What they desired they sought, and fortunately, they were literary, scholarly, artistic, and scientific as well as frivolous. Their passion for a well-groomed countryside changed the face of England; their love of building adorned it with an extraordinary architectural heritage; their mania for collecting endowed England with an incomparable artistic heritage; their addiction to sport enriched the world. And of all societies until our own, the aristocracy of eighteenth-century England was the most permissive. Theirs was the pursuit of happiness.

On a floating pleasure barge, the numerous kinsme

f William Sharp (topmost figure), surgeon to George III, hold a musical party on the Thames opposite Fulham, now an unfashionable London neighborhood.

The essence of comedy is the

triumph of *la forza di natura* — nature over intellect.

And the happiest tale

of all is the odyssey that ends with . . .

Laughter in the House

Gamboling Renaissance carnival figures adorn a 1575 edition of Petronius's Satyricon.

To begin with, the Happy Ending. Aristotle calls it the essential joy of comedy, and gives this example: mortal enemies of tragic drama confront, but suddenly convert. Instead of dueling to the death, Orestes and Aegisthus make friends and stroll happily off-stage. "Nobody kills anybody," Aristotle adds almost ruefully. Indeed, in the typical comic denouement, High Noon turns magically into lunchtime.

It has been this way since the dawn of Western literature, which is to say, since Homer. The *Iliad* defines the action of the tragic hero. First, a question of honor ignites the uncompromising wrath of Achilles and estranges him from the rest of the Greeks. Later, when his only friend, Patroclus, is killed, he is cut off from everything human. He refuses to eat or drink, and broods obsessively on the fated brevity of his life. He has grim consolation in the knowledge that his "glory" will live after him. Yet never once does he think of his wife or of the son who will fall heir to this glory. Even Sophocles' Ajax does this much before his death. So does Hector, the social hero Homer presents as a contrast to Achilles. Hector, the defender

of Troy, fights not for himself but for the preservation of family and society. Achilles has no such concerns, and as the *Iliad* ends, he has moved so far from mankind that he becomes merely "inhuman fire."

The fire of the *Odyssey* is quite the opposite; it is heart and hearth and the cooking of supper. This is our first comedy, and the only joys it presents are the joys of this world. But at the outset its hero is isolated from all earthly ties. We first glimpse Odysseus at the farthest point from humanity, on an island in the midst of nowhere, at "the navel of the sea." Though he is here with the nymph Calypso, he longs to leave, to struggle to regain homeland and home, wife and son. For this mortal domestic existence, he is even willing to sacrifice the eternity of transcendental bliss that Calypso offers:

Regal goddess, don't be angry with me. I know what you've said is right, and that in appearance careful Penelope is less imposing than you, and her stature less to look at. But then she is human and you immortal and immutable. And yet I desire—and long for always—to come home to my house, and to see the fruitful day of my returning.

Achilles forswears precisely what Odysseus desires. He abandons the world to gain an eternal intangible, whereas Odysseus makes the opposite journey for the temporal tangible.

The *Iliad* concludes with a funeral, the initial event in what will be the complete disintegration of a society. The flames that consume the pyre of Hector prefigure the burning of Troy. The *Odyssey* ends with a complete integration of society. Odysseus becomes a father again, embracing Telemachus by the light of the swineherd's fire, then a husband again, as Penelope joins him at his own hearth. Finally, after a symbolic remarriage, Odysseus fully re-enters the family structure when he again becomes his father's son. Appropriately, when he reveals himself to the aged Laertes, they embrace and then go into the house—to have dinner. This comic resolution contrasts sharply with what doubtless took place in Achilles' homeland, for old Peleus was never to see his son again, nor Neoptolemus his father.

The *Odyssey* explicitly rejects Iliadic values, especially the notion that otherworldly glory is in any way glorious.

By ERICH SEGAL

Even Achilles changes his mind. In Book 11, when Odysseus hails him as mightiest among the dead, Achilles retorts bitterly that there is *nothing* in death, that he would rather be a live peasant than a dead king. He then immediately asks about his son and about his father. The Odyssean Achilles speaks the philosophy of the entire poem, which, simply stated, is "Give me life."

Not coincidentally, these are the words Falstaff uses to justify his hasty retreat from the battle at Shrewsbury Field. In comedy, where hedonism replaces heroism, Falstaff is a genius, and Hotspur, so like Achilles in his thirst for glory, is a fool. As Fat Jack reasons:

What is honor? A word. What is that word honor? Air. A trim reckoning! Who hath it? He that died a Wednesday. Doth he feel it? No. Doth he hear it? No. 'Tis insensible then? Yea, to the dead.

If the tragic hero dies for what is nobler in the mind, the comic hero lives for what is livelier in the flesh. Hotspur cares for such intangibles as "bright honor," and would rather die than see his reputation sullied:

I better brook the loss of brittle life
Than those proud titles thou hast won of me.

The tragic hero prefers death to loss of name, the comic hero prefers life, however anonymous. Odysseus, Lord of Ithaca, Trojan War hero, sacker of many cities and renowned adventurer, forswears these titles and tells the hungry anthropophagus Cyclops he is no heroic morsel. In fact, he insists, "my name is Nobody." Better to be shamefully *hors de combat* than famously someone's hors d'oeuvre. Thus Falstaff retreats shouting "give me life," while Hotspur stands fast and becomes "food for worms."

Comedy's happy ending is exclusively human. The notion of a "divine comedy" is a contradiction in terms. Thus it is impossible to accept Dante's argument that his poem is a *commedia* because it begins in Hell and

ends in Paradise. The joy he extols is of the mind, *il ben de l'intelletto*, with a characteristically medieval renunciation of the physical world. Even in his amorous poetry women are incorporeal, as, for example, in the canzone *"Donne ch'avete intelletto d'amore,"* "Ladies that have the *intellect* of love." Only mind matters.

In direct and deliberate contrast, Boccaccio's *Decameron* is the "human comedy." In fact, its opening words are *umana cosa è . . .* Dante's inspiration was *"la gloriosa donna della mia mente."* Boccaccio's inspiration was also feminine, but in the plural—and in the flesh. He addresses his *Decameron* to the *graziosissime donne* to whom he is grateful for "loving kisses, lovely hugs and delightful gettings-together." *Gloriosa? Si. Della mente? No.* In fact, the *Decameron* contains a charming defense for true (i.e., human) comedy in the form of a little tale, the only one told by Boccaccio *in propria persona*. The story not only illustrates the contrasting mentalities of the Middle Ages and the Renaissance but also demonstrates the basic action of comedy.

Once upon a time, says Boccaccio, there was a man in Florence named Filippo Balducci who lived happily with his beloved wife. They existed only to give each other joy. Suddenly she died, and Filippo was left alone with their two-year-old son. Disconsolate, he decides to flee the world and give himself to the service of God. After selling his earthly goods, he takes his son to live in a tiny cell atop Mount Asinaio. There may be no deliberate allegory here, but the extreme "medievality" of both cell and mountaintop are unmistakable. Father and son spend the days in constant prayer and fasting. Filippo is especially strict with his son's education:

He took supreme caution never to discuss anything of the temporal world or let his son see any of it, lest it distract him from his holy duty. Instead, he constantly discoursed to him about the glories of Life

Eternal, of God and of the saints. He taught him nothing but prayers.

Filippo occasionally goes to Florence for whatever simple supplies they need, always leaving his son behind. But when the boy is eighteen, the father, now old and weary, accepts his offer to come along to help. Filippo reasons that his son is by now so indoctrinated, so inured against "the things of the world," *le cose del mondo*, that he cannot possibly be corrupted. And so they go off together to the city.

The young man gapes with wonder at the splendors of civilization—palaces, mansions, churches. He asks what each thing is and his father explains. But then they encounter a group of young girls, all dressed up, en route from a wedding.

The young man asks what they are.

"Lower your eyes, son," says Filippo, "don't look. They're a bad thing," *"elle son mala cosa."*

To which the youth replies, "Oh? What are they called?"

Now Filippo is loath to impart to his son knowledge that might awaken any counterproductive inclination (*"alcuno inchinevole desiderio men che utile"*), and so he simply tells his son the girls are called "geese."

Then Boccaccio reports a miracle, *"maravigliosa cosa ad udire"*: the young man loses interest in the palaces, churches, and other points of local geography. Sweetly he asks, "Father dear, could you arrange for me to get one of those geese?"

The old man responds with the universal moan of a parent who realizes his child is no longer a child: *"Oimè!"* he cries, adding, "Shut up—they're a bad thing," *"taci—elle son mala cosa!"*

To which the innocent boy replies, "Gee, are bad things so well-built?" *"O son cosí fatte le male cose?"*

To which the father dourly avers, "Yes."

The lad says he can see nothing bad in geese. They seem infinitely more beautiful than the painted angels Filippo has always shown him.

Beware of the geese

These engravings are from an eighteenth-century French edition of the *Decameron*. At left, a father tells his innocent son that the girls they see are really geese. At right, a canon gets his comeuppance from his bishop, who discovers him in bed with a servant woman. Opposite: A man revives a woman mistakenly interred, giving life to her unborn child as well; a jealous husband, attired in his wife's clothes to await her lover, is thrashed by him; and a couple make love in church while the husband they are cuckolding does penance.

The bishop's discovery

"Let me take one home, Father. I want to feed it."

"I refuse! You don't even realize *where* they have to be fed!" *"Tu non sai donde elle s'imbeccano!"* At this point, Filippo has to accept a basic truth that is Boccaccio's philosophy and comedy's law: *"E sentí incontanente piú aver di forza la natura che il suo ingegno."* "And instantly he realized that the force of nature was much stronger than his own contrivance."

Comedy is always the triumph of *la forza di natura.* What a contrast to the anticomic outlook of the Middle Ages, when Saint Thomas Aquinas's injunction was an absolute law of the Church: suppress all sensual feelings by force of reason. Boccaccio's little story shows the futility of even legislated abstinence. *La forza di natura* will always prevail, and this is precisely what human comedy presents: the triumph of instinct over intellect.

For what I call instinct may be substituted libido, *lebende Kraft,* life-force, Bergson's *élan vital,* or Schopenhauer's erotic "will," as in *The World as Will and Idea,* where comedy is viewed as "the arousal of a continued yes-saying to the will to live." Freudians might prefer to define comedy as the id's victory over the superego. This is especially apt in the case of Filippo Balducci since the superego is a precipitate of prohibitions imposed by parental authority. By whatever name, instinct is not only a will to live, but to produce life. Comedy is essentially erotic; *la forza di natura* is the healthy sexual appetite of Filippo's son, an urge that can overwhelm everything—even death.

A second story further illustrates this vital aspect of comic triumph: the tale of the Matron of Ephesus in Petronius's *Satyricon.* This account has a further dimension, since, like Chaucer, Petronius also describes the reaction of the audience to whom it is told, here a group of sailors on a voyage. When her husband suddenly dies, a young woman of Ephesus renowned for her piety is so grief-stricken that she follows the funeral procession into his tomb and remains weeping by the corpse. Five days pass. She will not eat or drink. Her servant can do nothing but sit silently as her mistress grieves to death.

Meanwhile, certain criminals have been crucified not far from the tomb. Guards are stationed to prevent relatives from stealing the bodies. Night falls. The single soldier on duty gazes across the cemetery and sees *"lumen inter monumenta clarius fulgens,"* "a light shining brightly among the tombs." His natural curiosity impels him to investigate, and he discovers the beautiful mourner. Deeply moved, he brings his meager supper into the tomb and offers it to her. She refuses, but her maidservant cannot. And, having eaten, she joins the soldier's attempts to persuade her mistress. She even quotes Virgil, "Do you think shades and ashes can really *feel* anything?"

At last the woman relents and eats, a step back toward life. The soldier begins a second campaign, again abetted by the maid. Here, too, the result is felicitous: *"ne hanc quidem partem*

corporis mulier abstinuit," "nor did the woman abstain with that part of her body either."

Then, and on nights thereafter, the bright glow is not seen across the tombs. The door has been shut while the lovers consummate their passion, *nuptias fecerunt.* But the family of one of the crucified criminals seizes the occasion to steal his body. The next morning the soldier emerges from the tomb, only to realize that he himself will be condemned to death. Rather than await judicial sentence, he will act the noble Roman and fall on his sword.

Now it is the woman's turn to preach life. She offers to sacrifice her husband's corpse to preserve her lover's body. At her insistence, they substitute the dead man for the stolen criminal. Here, *eros* literally triumphs over *thanatos* in the spirit of Petronius, whose entire work is infused with the doctrine of "give me life." The Woman of Ephesus fable has been told in many tongues and times; there is even a parallel in a Chinese Buddhist novella. La Fontaine caps his version with the moral *"mieux vaut goujat debout qu'empereur enterré,"* "a lackey on his feet outranks an emperor in his grave," echoing Achilles' very words to Odysseus, the quintessential comic credo!

There are many similarities between the tales of the Woman of Ephesus and Boccaccio's Filippo Balducci. Both celebrate the triumph of *la forza di natura,* the victory of instinct over intellect. And we note that instinct tends to center near the stomach, especially "that part of the body" the soldier

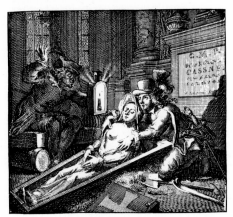

Raised from the dead

Lover's revenge

Unholy love

afterward attends to. But then, there is that distinctive feature of the Woman of Ephesus tale, the reaction of the audience: *"Risu excepere fabulam nautae."* "The sailors greeted the tale with *laughter."*

All comedy aspires to laughter, although not all laughter is related to comedy. Still, many essential aspects of comedy find affirmation in this response. To begin with, as Aristotle long ago observed, laughter is a uniquely human prerogative. Even that staid and serious Roman scholar Pliny justified his occasional reading of comedy, saying *"aliquando praeterea rideo . . . homo sum."* "Indeed, I laugh now and then. After all, I'm human." Psychologically, laughter signals the triumph of instinct over intellect. Or in Suzanne Langer's words, it is "the crest of a wave of felt vitality." And laughter is universally recognized as a social gesture, one that binds the community and integrates the society.

Legends of many cultures link laughter and fertility. In one Greco-Egyptian myth the beginning was not the Word, but the Laugh—and the Laugh was God. According to Apache legend, when the first man awakened to discover the first woman beside him, he spoke. Then she spoke. He laughed. Then she laughed. And as they went off together, the world burst into springtime and song. Theirs was a laughter of eros that set the world in bloom, as in the Homeric hymn to Demeter depicting a spring so intense that "The entire earth and all the salty sea laughed for joy."

Moreover, when Demeter loses Persephone, she not only refuses food and drink, but she is ἀγέλαστος, unlaughing. Then the earth starves, the flowers wilt, the fields are barren. The world is winter until mother and daughter are joyfully reunited.

Here on a cosmic level, we can see the same association between fertility and laughter evident in the Biblical tale of Sarah, who thus responded when told she would conceive at the age of ninety. Hence, it is understandable that apotropaic or mimetic fertility rites in widely diverse cultures feature laughter. And observers have been quick to note that ritual laughter expresses not merely the life-force but rebirth as well. This may even be seen in the famous Easter Laughter of the Greek Orthodox Church, which welcomes the resurrection of Christ.

And finally, the Happy Ending. What we have distinguished as the essential feature of comedy is strongly related to what has been called "elemental laughter," i.e., that of a newborn child. As early as Darwin, scientists have observed that a baby's first laugh is likely to occur when, after a brief separation from his mother, he sees her return. Thus the elemental laugh is related to the elemental happy ending: the reunion of the family, as in the Odyssean archetype. There appears to be a curious human need for this kind of simple resolution. Aristotle saw the happy ending not merely as pleasure for the audience, but one for which they collectively longed. Perhaps it is here ap-

propriate to recall Freud's observation that the essential comic pleasure lies in the temporary re-creation of the psychic state of childhood.

There is a short poem by Catullus that beautifully expresses this basic but complex delight. The poet has been journeying in far-off places and finally returns to his native village. Catullus hails the region and its lake in loving and erotic terms. After the anxieties of separation, he can now rest on the bed he dreamed of:

O what is more glorious than when, with cares unwinded, the mind sets down its baggage, and worn out from the efforts of travel, we come to our home and rest softly on our longed-for bed?

This vision, at once infantile and erotic, promises the twofold satisfaction that "homecoming" evokes in our imagination. It contains also the essence of comedy's happy ending. And see how Catullus in the final line asks to be welcomed by his beloved home: *"ridete quicquid est domi cachinnorum."* "Laugh out all the joyous laughter in the house!"

Comedy, then, is an odyssey from estrangement abroad to reunion at home. And the happiest of all possible endings is . . . laughter in the house.

This essay is from The Death of Comedy, *soon to be published by Harper & Row. Erich Segal is also the author of* Roman Laughter: The Comedy of Plautus *and the editor of a volume of essays on Euripides. He is now a visiting professor at the University of Munich.*

ROGER WOOD

LEPTIS MAGNA

This satellite city in North Africa once provided Rome with wheat and wild animals—the makings of bread and circuses. Today it is the best preserved relic of ancient Roman glory

I would recommend that any student of the past save up Leptis Magna to the last. As a sight, as an experience, there is nothing to equal it: it satisfies completely. The Parthenon is very fine, but coming back to it, time and again over the years, I find its very perfection boring. After twenty years of looking at the ruins of Rome, I have come to agree with the most ignorant tourist—they are sadly battered. Leptis Magna is perfect. It has splendor; it is as complete as any reasonable man could wish for; the restorers have been happily hampered by political convulsions and lack of funds; and above all, you can walk in its ruins for days on end, as I have done, and see nobody. I say this now, and I am only too well aware that,

At the theatre of Leptis Magna, opposite, a North African seaport conquered by Rome in 23 B.C., *descendants of Phoenicians sat in a semicircle watching the Roman comedies of Terence and Plautus. The foreground columns stand behind a 150-foot-long stage. Built in* A.D. *1–2 by a wealthy citizen, the theatre, like all the public buildings of Leptis Magna, was of purely Roman design.*

in a decade, I could sound ridiculous.

To see it, one must go to Tripoli, the most repellently ugly city on the shores of the Mediterranean. But the visit need last for one night only. One drives out early the next morning on the road to Homs, with the sea on the left and gray-green olive groves on the right. Then, later, searching fingers of sand, like little flows of golden lava, begin to snake between the trees and even spill upon the road. This is the sand of the desert, the sand that buried Leptis Magna after the Romans had gone, both those Romans of the Western Empire and those of Byzantium, and after the Vandals had torn down as much of the city as they had time and energy to do. They knocked down a number of the marble and sandstone columns, but after that Leptis was left in peace, to sleep in the African sun, under its blanket of sand. Some columns have been taken away during the centuries. Some are in the church of Saint-Germain-des-Prés in Paris; others can be found on the royal estate at Windsor in England. But these were minor robberies. Leptis, now that the sand is slowly being dug away, re-

By AUBREY MENEN

95

mains the most complete city to come down to us from the ancient world.

From the first glimpse of it, its sheer size overwhelms you. It was founded by the Phoenicians in the tenth century B.C., and as was their custom, they chose a promontory that sheltered a harbor. But it grew mightily, spreading along the shores like a river of stone. It was built of marble and sandstone, and the centuries have turned it into a city of amber—from the patina that has spread over its stones. Sometimes, when the sun is right, and when it is seen from the sea, it looks like a legendary city built of gold.

The city has only vestiges of walls, which are still under excavation. You enter through a great arch, standing by itself, that was put up on the orders of the boy from Leptis who had become emperor, Septimius Severus. It is tempting to think it was built to commemorate his returning in pomp and majesty to his native town, but we have no certain evidence that he ever went back. What we do know is that he gave orders that the town be beautified on an imperial scale. This arch is the first proof we meet that his orders were obeyed.

It has four entrances, flanked by elegant Corinthian columns. These were crowned by pointed triangular cornices, heavily carved, which have been found. They lent the arch a bold, thrusting liveliness, and break, successfully, the rules of classical architecture. Nobody can tell where this new idea came from, but perhaps it was from this very region. To this day, houses in the interior have decorations very like them, but much smaller. They are intended to ward off the evil eye.

Beside the arch, buried in the sand, were found huge reliefs. Remarkably well preserved, they show Septimius Severus with his two sons, Caracalla and Geta, performing various ceremonies: he is seen riding in a triumphal chariot and sacrificing at a temple with his head covered by a veil, as ritual prescribed. There is an extremely vivid portrayal of the sacrificial bull being slaughtered amid a great crowd of

From one end of the theatre stage the figure of a Dioscurus, one of the twin sons of Leda and Zeus, gazed out on the Leptis audience.

courtiers, all rendered with brilliant realism. So is the emperor. He has a broad face with large, expressive eyes that are turned upward in a haughty stare over the heads of his subjects. He is heavily bearded, but that does not conceal thick, fleshy lips that curve skeptically downward. It is the exact rendering of the man who once remarked that he had seen everything and done everything and it was all worth nothing much.

The arch gives onto a paved street lined with mounds that are still not excavated but that contain houses. This long perspective ends in another arch, a very simple one, with a rounded top, built by the emperor Tiberius, in whose reign Jesus died. On either side of this lie the principal ruins of Leptis Magna in all their splendor.

We pass under another arch, this time built by Trajan. It, too, has columns, but the contrast between it and the flamboyant arch of Septimius Severus is striking. Here, with Trajan, all is classical, restrained, and orderly. Even the molding of the bases of the column tells a different tale. Those of the Trajan arch are almost delicate; those of Septimius Severus are heavy and bold. Seventy-six years separate the two reigns, and it is clear that a profound change in taste had taken place. Walk-

ing between them, I felt I could detect the first sign of that unbridled willfulness that, as soon as Severus died, was to sweep over the Roman Empire and reduce it to chaos.

But we must not forget that these were Semitic people, living in a town founded for trade and growing rich by trade. This was an independent Punic city, save for a brief period under a Numidian king, Massinissa, until it was finally subdued by the Romans in 23 B.C. But for all their Roman masters, Leptis was built and adorned by its citizens. They left their names inscribed on stone to remind us, and the list tells their story: Iddibal, Ithymbal, Annobal, Ammicar, Balithon, Boncarth, Muthumbal, Bodmelquart, Himilcho, and Byrycth—all of them men of Punic stock.

The heart of the city, inevitably, was the market place. It is a great paved space supporting a forest of columns, over a hundred of them, and many complete. As befits a place of such importance, it was approached by an elaborate portico and securely walled round, like a fortress. Once inside those walls, all was charm and lightness. A columned walk ran around all four of them. In the center were two octagonal pavilions, the roof supported on the outside by columns and in the middle by a second, circular pavilion pierced by arches. There can be no doubt that these were the auricle and ventricle of Leptis: the citizens erected monuments to their most distinguished leaders hard beside them. We have only the bases left, stone models of a four-way arch, on which were put honorific chariots of bronze. On one of them is carved a more direct and blunt reminder of where the citizens' money came from—two excellent reliefs of ships, one with a sail and one without.

In the market place, too, is the block of stone that controlled the weights, also of stone. There are depressions into which the weights had to fit with accuracy. Another stone has lines upon it that helped in converting one linear measure into another, as useful to foreigners as the currency tables we carry around with us today on our travels.

Even the hangers-on who frequent every market place have left a memorial—the porters, the errand boys, the idlers ready to snatch a tip or two for some light service. On a stone step are the holes they used for playing some game to pass the moments when business was slack.

From the market, it is only a few steps to the place where the tired businessmen relaxed, the theatre. It is down by the shore, so that spectators in the top rows got a view of the Mediterranean. The semicircle of stone seats descends to a wall, beyond which is a curved platform for the chairs of the chief men of the city. In front of this is a semicircular space with the base of an altar in the middle. Beyond this rises the stage, fifty yards long and nine yards wide, quite untouched since the day it was discovered. Behind this again, rises the *scaena,* the permanent background to the performance.

To any actor, and to any producer, this setting breathes "theatre." To any tourist board, it breathes money, and what is more, a solution to that vexing problem of what the tourist is to do in the evening. So each summer, in many of the surviving Roman theatres, classical plays are put on. Since you cannot charge high prices for stone or wooden seats, the actors are second-rate. Since we have not the least idea of how the chorus of a classical play behaved, the girls and boys of the local dance academy are called upon to prance about in various postures thought by the producer, on no basis whatever, to be classical. Music is added, very Greek, though not a single fragment of Greek music has survived. The performances are given at night because the producers cannot tear themselves away from electric light, although all classical performances were given in the daytime. The result has about as much connection with antiquity as a coronation procession put on at the Radio City Music Hall would

In the last row of the theatre, Ceres, goddess of agriculture, and the child she holds, took their places as if they were playgoers.

have with the history of the British monarchy.

When all this started, I was inclined to consider it harmless, and sometimes quite funny. Now I am not so sure. The first problem is that it is a dangerous thing to stumble about ruins at night. Tourists must be protected from twisting an ankle or breaking a leg. The ruins, *ergo,* must be made rather less ruinous. A few slabs here, a few blocks there ("it *must* have been like this") and the place is made safe. The stage, too, though picturesque, is inconvenient and not to the modern taste. A column moved here, one set up there ("well, it belongs, doesn't it?") and the producer gets his effects much better. Loose stones lying about are an impediment. Moving them a few feet can do no harm. Actors dislike suddenly disappearing down holes in the stage, or elsewhere. Repaving ("with the same stone the Romans used, mind you") is called for.

This has not happened at Leptis Magna. When the archaeologists cleared it from the sand, they found that a number of its columns had been thrown down, whether by an earthquake or an invader it was difficult to say. But they had fallen in their places and could safely be re-erected. Some statues were also discovered. They were not carried

off to the museums (though there would be reason for doing so) but, with great good sense, they were put back on their pedestals. The theatre is wonderfully complete, without any faking. No producer has felt the itch to produce "his" Sophocles there, and never will. Leptis is too remote to attract an audience, except, perhaps, of camel drivers.

But in antiquity audiences were large, and the tired businessman of Leptis was well catered to. On great occasions the great tragedies would have been performed; at other times, there would be the comedies of Plautus and Terence, in which the citizens would see themselves portrayed on the stage, usually without flattery. The performance of any play, whether tragedy or comedy, was utterly unlike anything we see today. For one thing, the actors, who wore masks, usually faced the audience. They could, if they wished, turn away, but the principal speeches were delivered frontally. All depended on two things: the beauty of the actor's declamation, and his gestures. In the declamation, clearness was everything: Vitruvius remarks, like a schoolmaster teaching Latin today, that the case endings of words must not be mumbled.

Companies of mimes toured the empire and were immensely popular. They wore no masks, they often improvised (though texts were sometimes written for them), and their humor was low. They were dressed in hoods, which could be drawn over their heads or flung back. Beneath this was a simple tunic to which was attached a leather phallus, which, by means of a string, could be erected at a suitable point in the stories they told. Their favorite themes were adultery and homosexuality, but they varied these with topical allusions, often of a biting nature. In a commercial city like Leptis, it is easy to see that the mimes would be very welcome.

There is a fine view of Leptis from the top row of the theatre, and it is a view of columns, row upon row of them, stretching out into the distance. It seems, at first, that there are too many columns in Leptis, too many porticoes, too many columned walks lining the streets. But it is this that makes Leptis an instructive ruin. Columns fall down easily; once down, they are simple to cut up. In all the other cities that antiquity has left us, this has happened to a degree. Chance may have preserved the columns of a temple, but it rarely has spared the porticoes that surrounded it. They were, however, a vital part of any town built in the time of the Greeks and the Romans.

Porticoes were probably a Greek invention. A porch, or stoa, was built in the agora at Athens where philosophers could talk. Eventually a philosophy arose that took its name from the place. The Stoics came to Rome and made a living by teaching in, once more, the porches. Porticoes and colonnades sprang up all over the empire. They were so popular that rich men felt it essential to have porticoes in their own villas. They were built around the garden in the heart of the house. In Pompeii I have often walked in them, thinking, always, that no better idea for a Mediterranean dwelling had ever been thought of. The Middle Ages agreed with me. These private porticoes came back in the shape of monastery cloisters.

Besides their porticoes, the citizens of Leptis had another meeting place. It stands a short distance away from the theatre, its yellow walls, built of huge blocks of stone, still upright. From the inside, it looks like a cathedral without a roof. Immense columns with deeply carved capitals line the walls. At one end is an apse with two columns even bigger than those in the nave. Everywhere there is rich decoration, intricate tendrils weaving about stone medallions portraying legends. It is a masterly piece of architecture, one of the finest in the whole empire, but one's first, overwhelming impression on entering it is wonder at the vast amount of money it must have cost. It is the basilica, and it was also a present from Septimius Severus to his home town.

The basilica was the court of law of the city. The apse was for the judge. When it was new, the basilica had an upper gallery. This was for the spectators, who could also crowd the great nave to listen. We have no record of the procedure there, but we have ample evidence of what went on in the basilicas at Rome. There could have been little difference, for the Romans imposed their legal proceedings on all their subjects, allowing them to keep only such of their own laws as suited Roman imperial convenience.

The Romans attached so much importance to *gravitas*—a dignified, self-controlled, grave manner—that it might be thought that trials were conducted with the hushed solemnity of the Supreme Court or the British Courts of Justice. It was quite the reverse. Trials were sometimes abandoned because of the sheer noise and confusion.

In the time of the Roman Republic, cases were pleaded by prominent men, such as senators, and they were strictly forbidden to accept fees. By the time of Septimius Severus (and before) such high-mindedness had been discarded. Cases were still argued by prominent people—it was an essential step in a political career—but these men did take fees, and, as now, they were high ones.

Some knowledge of the law was essential, of course, to argue a case, but it was not the most important thing. Counsel had to have a fine voice and a gift of rhetoric. He expected, and was given, free play. The more he embroidered his theme, the better he was considered to be. The orators often carried this to a degree that exasperated the litigant. Martial puts it very succinctly: "You," he says to his counsel, "with a mighty voice and every gesture you know, make the Court ring with Cannae and Mithridatic War, and insensate Punic perjuries and Sullas, and Mariuses and Muciuses. Now mention, Postumus, my three she-goats."

The basilica at Leptis, like many others, has survived by a turn of fate. When Christianity became legal in the Roman Empire, under Constantine, the Christians had no churches. They met in one another's houses. When they were free to build, they confronted a problem. The only places of worship in existence were the hated pagan temples. They could not be copied, and in any case, they were not designed for the Christian ritual. The basilicas were, however, ideal. The altar was placed in front of the apse, the bishop sat where the judge had sat, and the congregation gathered in the wide space between the walls. When this grew too small, transepts were added left and right of the altar to take care of the overflow. Thus the design for Christian churches was established. The four great pilgrimage churches of Rome still bear the name of the Roman courts of law.

It is to this fact that we owe the preservation of the great basilica of Leptis. When the Roman Empire became Christianized, the basilica became a church. With capitals looted from other buildings, the Leptis Christians built a pulpit. It lies, now, in ruins. But that was the only thing they did to the building. The basilica has come down to us otherwise untouched, the finest relic of its kind in the whole Roman world.

So much of the harbor of Leptis Magna is left that it could be made usable again today. Ships could tie up to its bollards, were there any water; goods could be loaded and unloaded on the harbor steps; and, with the aid of some roofs, the goods could be stored in the warehouses. The site is as evocative as Pompeii.

It lies between two headlands, each crowned with massive ruins that jut out

Four mosaic strips from Leptis, opposite, commemorate a deadly Roman sport, gladiatorial combat. In the top two panels an orchestra is providing background music for a fight to the death. The bottom two panels show prisoners from Leptis serving as live human bait to attract leopards, lions, and other beasts from the African hinterland. These were exported to Rome, where the rich advertised their affluence by keeping them in private zoos and the poor watched them being slaughtered in the Colosseum.

boldly into the sea, the waves beating and breaking against the gigantic stones of their foundations. Between them lies what was once the harbor. It is silted up now, and covered with bushes. You cross this as though you were a ship. Before you, rising as you walk, is the long quay. Stone steps run down to the water level, so unworn and so complete that they look as though they have hardly been used. Indeed, the whole quay is so fresh-looking that the archaeologists were driven to put forward a theory. They surmised that shortly after Septimius Severus had it built, the trade of Leptis suffered a sharp recession from which it never recovered.

Certainly something strange happened. The stone bollards that line the edge barely show the marks of the hawsers of the ships that were tied to them. Behind them runs a colonnade, and the columns seem fresh from the chisel. We shall probably never know the reason. Men do not put up inscriptions to record a slump in trade.

The trade on which the merchants of Leptis depended and which made them rich was with Rome, the capital of the known world. Rome was the center of their thoughts, the subject of their conversations, the source of their hopes and fears. It was to Rome that they went to make their bargains, sailing in their famous ships to Brindisi or Naples, jolting up the Appian Way in four-wheeled carriages or swaying litters. It was in Rome that they picked up the news and gossip they would retail back in Leptis.

The exports of Leptis to Rome consisted chiefly of three things: olive oil, wheat, and wild beasts for the amphitheatre. Romans could not live and be happy without these commodities. We all learned at school that the emperors kept the people of Rome content with "bread and circuses." The "bread,"

Staring up from the rubble, the medallion opposite, bearing the face of a sea nymph, once adorned an arcaded portico built by Septimius Severus, an urban amenity the Romans extended throughout the empire.

Rome's goddess of victory, as lovely as her legions were fierce, adorned an arch built to honor the emperor Severus, a native of Leptis.

with which went olive oil, was a dole.

Scholars will never cease arguing about how many people lived in Rome in imperial times, but the best guess is that it was over a million, a gigantic mob for those days when there were far fewer people in the world. For a great number of them, there was nothing to do and no way of earning steady money. The emperors solved the problem in a thoroughly modern way. They taxed the empire without mercy and gave the money away to the citizens. This form of social security was concealed by making the donations on occasions for rejoicing—a victory, the birth of an imperial son, and so forth. They backed this up by making sure that the permanently unemployed had at least something to eat. Permits were issued to enable them to have free bread and oil. This applied to only a part of the population; at its peak, the dole catered for no more than 320,000 people. Enough, however, to keep Leptis rich.

The parallel with the dole of our own times helps us, in a very rough way, to understand the free distribution of bread and oil. When it comes to the circuses, we are completely at sea. We can perhaps have sympathy with the quarter of a million Romans who regularly packed the Circus Maximus to watch the chariot racing. But when we realize that fifty thousand as regularly went to the Colosseum to watch gladi-

ators slaughter one another, or cheer mock naval battles that were imitations in all respects save that the participants were actually killed, then we must confess that we do not understand.

The good merchants of Leptis did a brisk trade in wild beasts, caught in the African hinterland by hunters, caged and shipped from the great harbor of Leptis and other Punic towns along the coast, and sold at high prices to eager buyers in the capital. The Romans had a vivid interest in wild animals, the more exotic the better. They were fond of elephants, whom they thought sagacious. They marveled at giraffes; they made pets of jaguars and leopards (the emperor Elagabalus used to bring them to sit at his table among his guests). In a way, these beasts were a mark of Empire, like the Indian princes who were paraded at Queen Victoria's jubilees. To the ordinary man in the Forum, the strange animals were proof that he really ruled the world.

They also liked to see animals killed. Man is a hunter, and there is nothing to be done about it; but only the Romans turned the hunting of animals into a spectator sport. The Colosseum was tastefully decorated with trees and bushes so that it resembled a forest. Hundreds of wild animals were then let out of the dark dungeons underneath into the full glare of the Roman sun. Huntsmen shot them down, to the huge enjoyment of spectators who did not lift a finger except to clap their hands. Sometimes the emperor would stand up in his royal box, take a bow or a javelin, and dispatch a few beasts himself, carefully protected by barriers, nets, and huntsmen ready to destroy any animal so lacking in respect as to try to leap at the master of the world.

Not all the emperors were marksmen, but all gave wild beast shows to please their subjects. Augustus Caesar was a pacific man who wore long flannel underwear and liked playing simple games with cheerful little boys. He gave twenty-six wild animal displays. Thirty-five hundred animals were killed. This was before the Colosseum was built, so

This headless statue of a seated woman decorated a street in the center of the city.

things were on a modest scale. Titus dedicated the great structure with one hundred days of spectacle. Nine thousand animals died. There was better to come. Standing to this day in Rome is a sculptured column on which is portrayed Trajan's victory over the Dacians. But the Romans needed something more exciting than bas-reliefs. He gave 123 days of shows. Eleven thousand animals died.

All this was very good for business in Leptis: wild animals were consumer goods that had constantly to be replaced. There were variants of the mass slaughter. Expert men, armed with daggers or javelins, were hired to fight particularly ferocious animals. Some of these men became quite famous, and the merchants of Leptis paid tribute to them. A fresco has been unearthed there. It shows ten of these heroes, four of them being sufficiently celebrated to have their names written beside them. They are fighting six leopards and, with sporting impartiality, three of these beasts are named: Rapidus, Fulgentius, and Gabatius. One wonders what brought them this honor: perhaps in previous combats they had always brought down their man. The leopard Rapidus, I am sorry to say, is about to be killed.

Martial has a vivid description of one animal entertainment that must have been designed to glut the most avid sadists among the spectators. A condemned criminal was led out to a cross in the middle of the arena and crucified. Then a famished bear was turned loose. This entertainment had very little artistry. Others were designed with more taste. Nero had a considerable sense of the theatre, as we know from the performances he gave as a singer. He astonished his subjects by actually descending from the imperial box, armed only with a club, and boldly facing a lion. He killed it. The lion had, of course, been drugged, but it all made a pretty picture.

As long as Rome could afford its bread and circuses, Leptis prospered. But when this lucrative trade began to dry up, the decline of the North African city came swiftly. Leptis, too, had its barbarians on the frontier. They were the tribes in the interior. For a long time the legions kept them at bay. But as the power of Rome decreased, the boldness of the tribesmen grew. Leptis was attacked repeatedly. At last came the Vandals, sweeping into Africa and founding a kingdom.

The new Rome, at Constantinople, sent an army that defeated them. Belisarius, the victorious general, put a wall around the harbor so that his communications with Constantinople would be safe, but the rest of the city was neglected. The sands began to take over. Here, too, came the Arabs, but Leptis by now was semiabandoned. By a coincidence, it was Justinian who raised the last building we can see in Leptis. It is thought to be a Christian church. It is now no more than walls built of large blocks, and some arches. But it is built of reused stones, a sign that, even then, there were ruins in Leptis Magna.

"Leptis Magna" is part of Aubrey Menen's forthcoming book Cities in the Sand, *to be published by Dial Press in mid-October. Author of* The Prevalence of Witches, *he is of Indian and Irish parentage, but considers himself most at home in Rome.*

The Mediterranean, mare nostrum *to the Romans, laps at the seaport of Leptis.*
The ancient harbor lies between the foreground ruins and the misty city beyond.

In 1880, when Vanity Fair *ran this drawing of him, Parnell was parliamentary chief of the Irish Nationalists.*

Kitty O'Shea and the Uncrowned King of Ireland

Thanks to the eloquence and political skill of Charles Parnell, Home Rule for Ireland was near victory by 1890. Then came the rumors, the denials, the squalid divorce. Irish independence had to wait a generation

"The uncrowned King of Ireland will sit at my table at the next dinner I give." So boasted Katherine O'Shea when her husband's colleagues in Parliament warned her of Charles Stewart Parnell's inaccessibility and dislike of social intercourse.

It was the summer of 1880. Gladstone and the Liberals were back in power at Westminster. But there was a new element in the House of Commons. This was Charles Parnell's Irish Nationalist party, the first strong and truly independent force for Irish Home Rule to emerge since the 1800 Act of Union had made Ireland an integral part of Great Britain. The British people had never recognized the wrongs done to the Irish peasantry by ruthless agents acting for absentee landlords. Tenant farmers were forced to hand over the whole of their produce—with the exception of the potato crop. The potato blight of the 1840's, which destroyed the entire crop, revealed the iniquity of the system. Thousands died of hunger. Those who were able, emigrated to America. Ireland became an impoverished and depopulated country where every despairing, abortive attempt at rebellion brought heavier measures of repression. By the 1870's the radical element among the English Liberals was beginning to show some sympathy for Ireland. A few even envisaged a mild form of local

Katherine Wood, an Englishwoman, was the wife of William O'Shea for twenty-three years and Parnell's mistress for ten of them.

government, but this scheme fell short of satisfying Parnell. His aim was nothing less than Home Rule for Ireland.

Katherine's husband, Captain William O'Shea, whose name was to be fatally linked with Parnell's, was the newly elected Nationalist member for County Clare. He was the son of a hard-working Dublin solicitor whose earnings had provided him with a good education and a commission in a

fashionable regiment. But he had failed to live up to his father's expectations. Vain, shiftless, forever in debt, he had resigned his commission on marrying in order to embark on a business career that invariably landed him in difficulties. His principal asset was his wife, whose influential relations were always pulling him out of scrapes.

She was entirely English. The thirteenth child of a titled parson, Katherine Wood had made what her relations considered a poor match in marrying the handsome, feckless young Irish captain. The first years of her married life were a long series of vicissitudes —one moment she had her own carriage and a French maid, the next she was nursing her sick husband in some dreary furnished room. The birth of three children added to her difficulties, and after nine years of marriage she was glad to accept the offer of a house and a fixed income from a rich old aunt who lived on a large estate at Eltham, on the outskirts of London.

By that time, Willie was involved in business that was always taking him off on trips abroad. In London he rented bachelor rooms in the Haymarket and visited his wife and children only on weekends. It was not a very satisfactory life for a spirited young woman in her thirties. But Mrs. Benjamin Wood—the octogenarian aunt—not only bought

Kitty's clothes but on occasion went so far as to pay the Captain's debts. For Katherine remained on amicable and even affectionate terms with her husband. She was convinced that, given a proper chance, Willie could still make a splendid career for them both.

In late 1879 the Captain's ambitions turned to politics: William O'Shea, M.P., would have a better chance of getting on in the financial world than plain Captain O'Shea. The election of 1880 gave him his opportunity. It was both easier and cheaper to get elected to an Irish seat than to an English one. The Nationalist party was notoriously short of cash, and anyone who contributed to the party funds and paid for his own electioneering expenses was welcome. Katherine, who was thrilled by the prospect of becoming a political hostess, succeeded in wheedling the necessary money out of "dear Aunt Ben," and Captain O'Shea was duly returned on the Home Rule ticket for West Clare.

On first meeting this new recruit, Parnell is reported to have said, "That's just the kind of man we do not want in the Party." But in that motley assortment of journalists and farmers, Ulster tradesmen and Dublin lawyers, no one was much bothered by inconsistencies. What could have been more incongruous than the elegant Mr. Parnell, the fox-hunting squire of Avondale, appearing on the same platform with Michael Davitt, a Mayo peasant who after the Fenian uprising of 1867 had served a term in Portland Jail? All that united them was a fierce hatred of British rule in Ireland—a hatred Parnell had inherited from his beautiful Irish-American mother. Delia Parnell had fed her children on Anglophobia from the cradle: two of her daughters were passionate Fenians, and her son Charles, a shy, undemonstrative boy, was caught up in a vortex of politics after the unsuccessful 1867 rebellion.

Patriotism and outraged pride made Parnell a Nationalist, and as such, in the eyes of Unionist landlords, a traitor to his class. By the age of thirty, this tall, slight young man with a pale face and deep-set, burning eyes was recognized as having the makings of a great leader. His speeches, delivered in a quiet monotone, contained more fire and passion than the greatest flights of oratory; the Honorable Member for Cork was more adulated, and more hated, than any other member of the British House of Commons. He was a lonely, reserved bachelor who discouraged the slightest intimacy. Whenever he could escape from politics, he retired to Ireland, to the woods of Avondale and the grouse moors of Aughavanagh.

Mrs. O'Shea's first attempts to meet the Irish leader were unsuccessful: her effusive notes elicited polite but negative replies. She refused, however, to take No for an answer. On a fateful summer's afternoon in 1880, when Parliament was in the throes of the first reading of the Irish Coercion Bill, Parnell was informed that two ladies who wished to speak to him were waiting in a carriage outside. The name on one of the cards was that of Mrs. O'Shea, the woman who had so persistently bombarded him with invitations. It was with a feeling of boredom and irritation that he stepped out into the sunlight of Westminster's Palace Yard.

She was quite different from what he had expected. Here was no strident, self-possessed female, but a shy, diffident young woman who blushed when she addressed him and whose smile radiated happiness and goodwill. There was warmth in the large brown eyes and gaiety in the round little face, with the curls clustering so thickly under the fashionable bonnet. Parnell never even noticed her sister, who was sitting beside her in the carriage, for he fell in love with Katherine at first sight. More than thirty years later, when she was a feeble old woman, she could still recapture the wonder of their first meeting, of how Parnell came out into Palace Yard, "a tall, gaunt figure, thin and deadly pale," and "how he looked straight at me with an intensity which made me think: 'This man is wonderful and different.'"

Within a week the "uncrowned King of Ireland" was the guest of honor at a dinner party given by the O'Sheas at Thomas's Hotel in London. Katherine had vindicated her pride and shown her husband's colleagues that her charms could succeed where those of so many had failed. The Captain already saw himself a rung higher on the political ladder, as Parnell's liaison with the Liberals.

On the day that Parnell fell in love with Mrs. O'Shea he became enmeshed in a web of lies and subterfuges. These pretenses meant nothing to Katherine, whose marriage had only survived by means of intrigues calculated to maintain the aura of respectability no woman could afford to neglect in Victorian society. For her, the important thing was to prevent any hint of scandal from reaching the ears of Aunt Ben. The old lady was eighty-six, and it could only be a few months or years before she died, leaving Kitty in possession of a large enough fortune to buy off her husband, ensure her children's future, and allow her to devote herself to a jealous and demanding lover.

Parnell had found at last a woman whom he not only loved but trusted. And for all her limitations, she never failed him in her love. She knew the dangers involved, but neither of them could resist taking every opportunity to meet, either at her sister's house or at the Westminster Palace Hotel, where he had a suite of rooms. They would take tea in his sitting room, and he would talk to her of things that interested him—politics, the condition of the Irish peasants, his experiments in mineralogy. He was not a witty or amusing man, but with her, there was no need to make conversation; indeed, there were times when he was so tired that his brain refused to function, and he would just lie on a sofa and listen to her bright, effortless chatter as she arranged the cushions behind his head and placed flowers in his gloomy rooms. They met chiefly in the House of Commons, when it was in session. There, Mrs. O'Shea was to be found every Wednesday afternoon in the Ladies' Gallery, introduced not by her husband but by Mr. Parnell—as reporters were quick to note. On summer evenings when there was no urgent business before the House, she could be seen leaving the building with Parnell. They would drive down to Richmond or Mortlake, dining in some small restaurant by the river, where Kitty always managed to invest the scene with a lyrical quality that enchanted Parnell.

While Mrs. O'Shea bent her efforts to preserving both her own and her husband's reputation, Parnell went so far as to beg her to divorce O'Shea and marry him, heedless of the fact that as the leader of a Catholic country he could never marry a divorced woman. Katherine asked him to have "just a little patience"; her aunt could not live much longer, and if they only waited, everything could be arranged without causing anyone unnecessary pain.

So long as her children's inheritance was uncertain, Katherine refused to divorce her husband; so long as there was money to be extorted from Aunt Ben, the Captain was careful not to create a scandal. Willie was never the injured husband he later claimed to be. Through Parnell, he had hoped to obtain a Cabinet post from the grateful Liberals, and his cynical advice to his wife had been to "take him back to Eltham and make him comfortable for the night." Kitty similarly found it natural to use her influence on her husband's behalf: "Willie can be useful," she assured Parnell when she begged him to find O'Shea a new constituency, for the electors of West Clare had made it clear they would never vote for him again.

In successive elections Parnell had to support the nomination of a man he hated and despised. But not even he could make the Orangemen of Armagh or the Irish voters of the Exchange Division of Liverpool accept the smooth-faced Captain. In one of the bitterest hours of his political career he had to force O'Shea on the townspeople of

KATHERINE WOOD PARNELL, *Charles Stewart Parnell*, NEW YORK, 1914

William O'Shea was a captain in the 18th Hussars, a fashionable regiment of the day.

Galway, against the wishes of some of of his principal lieutenants, one of whom sent him an open telegram saying: "Mrs. O'Shea will be your ruin."

From the autumn of 1880 they were lovers, and Mrs. O'Shea assures us in her memoirs that from then on Willie was her husband only in name, though when a child was born in the spring of 1882, Willie appears to have been convinced that he was the father.

The romance flowered against the background of growing political strife and violence. Parnell was constantly crossing over to Ireland, where he incited the people to resist eviction and the exorbitant demands of the landlords. "Ireland for the Irish and the land for the people!" was his party's rallying cry. His speeches became so subversive that government detectives shadowed him and censored his correspondence, so that his letters to Mrs. O'Shea had to be sent under cover to various addresses. The House of Commons became too public a meeting place; often, the lovers met in Waterloo Station, where Katherine would sit up half the night in the first-class waiting room, until Parnell could get away from the House. When he was to cross over to Ireland by the early morning boat train,

she would be waiting at the St. Pancras Hotel, having ordered a hot supper to be ready for him when he escaped from work so he could have a few hours' rest before catching the train.

Nothing that gave him a moment's pleasure was too much trouble. Even so, Kitty must have been somewhat panic-stricken when, at a time when Willie was away in Paris, Parnell appeared one night at Eltham to tell her he was in imminent danger of arrest, asking her to hide him for a fortnight, as if it was the easiest thing in the world to hide a grown man in a house full of children and servants. Somewhat unwisely, she consented.

On this occasion the lovers made their first serious mistake. Parnell left a portmanteau behind at Eltham, which, through the inadvertent indiscretion of a maid, was handed to O'Shea, who was thereby forced to play for the first time the role of jealous husband. It irked him to discover that his wife had lost her head to this dry, taciturn Irishman, who was, by Willie's standards, totally lacking in charm. The Captain was peculiarly sensitive about his reputation, and as yet had not received any material advantage to compensate for being made ridiculous in the eyes of his colleagues. But Kitty was in no mood to be lectured on morals by a husband who had been persistently unfaithful and who did not contribute so much as a bottle of whisky to the running of the household. In a moment of fury she confessed her love for Parnell. This cost her dearly, for it gave Willie an opportunity to exercise his talent for blackmail. His first move was to challenge Parnell to a duel, but he was horrified to find his opponent not only willing to fight but ready to suggest a meeting place at Boulogne. The gallant Captain had to resort to preying on his wife's fears in order to prevent a duel that would have been disastrous for both.

There was endless intriguing and bargaining, with Parnell trying to remain aloof from it all. For Kitty's sake, he paid out the sums O'Shea demanded, and it is believed that for several years

In 1886 Prime Minister Gladstone (standing) introduced the Irish Home Rule Bill in Parliament. Chiefly because of the outcry from Ulster—"Home Rule is Rome Rule"—it was rejected.

the Captain received an income of six hundred pounds a year from his wife's lover. Having bought Willie's silence, Parnell made little attempt to hide his dislike and contempt for him. A story is told of how one day when the three were staying together in Brighton and Katherine was chatting with her husband in her room, Parnell stalked in, white with rage, and without a word picked her up, threw her over his shoulder, and marched across the corridor into his own room, where he flung her onto his bed and slammed the door.

Katherine might pride herself on having obtained the "uncrowned King of Ireland" for her lover, but she still lived in continual anxiety and fear. For a delicate, high-strung man like Parnell, who throughout his life had suffered from nervous depressions, the strain must have been intolerable. Their child, a little girl born in the spring of 1882, when Parnell was a prisoner in Kilmainham Jail, was the first victim of the couple's emotional distress: sickly from birth, she died within a few months.

The Coercion Act of 1882 had left the government no other choice but to arrest Parnell, and though the Irish leader's treatment in prison was remarkably humane, his nerves could not stand the strain of confinement. Mrs. O'Shea took advantage of his weakness

—and of his longing to be with her and their sick child—to urge upon him the necessity of coming to terms with the British government, and, in return for certain concessions to the Irish farmers, to offer to help put down the widespread agrarian revolt in Ireland. For the first time Kitty stepped directly into the political arena, using her influence to make Parnell work for the solution that "she believed to be best for Ireland." The man she suggested as intermediary between Parnell and the Liberals was none other than her despised and contemptible husband.

It seems inexplicable that anyone could have trusted O'Shea. Yet even Gladstone, who at first was wary of these overtures, admitted in private that he "could not help feeling indebted to O'Shea." Joseph Chamberlain, the Radical member for Birmingham and a rising star on the political firmament, was willing not only to confer with the Irish Nationalists and offer them some form of self-government but to make use of O'Shea in negotiating with Parnell. This was the source of the fatal misunderstanding and bitter hatred that grew up between Chamberlain and the Irish leader. Had they met directly, each would have known how far the other was prepared to go. But the Captain, who was only concerned in pro-

moting himself, quoted promises Parnell had never made. In trusting O'Shea, Chamberlain showed a serious error of judgment that resulted in the splitting of the Liberal party, for while Chamberlain and the Liberal Unionists were never prepared to accept more than a form of Irish self-government, Gladstone, once committed to Home Rule, was ready to stake his political future on the issue.

Persuaded by Mrs. O'Shea, Parnell put his signature to the so-called Kilmainham Treaty. Outwardly he was the victor, and he was referred to in the House of Commons as "the greatest power in Ireland of the day." But in reality the Kilmainham Treaty struck the first blow at the independence of the Nationalist party, sapping the integrity of his associates, who one by one succumbed to the flattery of the Liberal "wirepullers" and the fascination of Gladstone, whom Parnell recognized from the beginning to be "more dangerous as a friend than as an enemy." At the same time, he knew that the septuagenarian statesman was the one man with sufficient prestige and courage to carry Home Rule through Parliament.

All hopes of an agreement vanished in the spring of 1882, when Lord Frederick Cavendish, the newly appointed Secretary for Ireland and one of the most popular figures in London society, was murdered by assassins while walking home with a colleague to his residence in Dublin's Phoenix Park. The news of this outrage shocked the world and started a wave of anti-Irish feeling in the country. Overnight, Parnell became the most hated man in England, and even the more moderate politicians believed him to be associated with anarchists and dynamiters. The bitterness of public feeling forced Gladstone to reintroduce coercion, though he secretly continued to work toward a better understanding with Ireland.

Parnell himself was probably the more deeply affected of the two. Previously his feelings toward the Fenians had been ambiguous: though he had never advocated violence, he had never spoken out against it. But now he was so shattered by these cruel and unnecessary murders that he seriously thought of retiring from politics, and he might well have done so had it not been for Kitty. From the year 1882 Mrs. O'Shea became increasingly important in Parnell's life, assuming the roles of mistress, mother, and nurse. Suspecting her husband of being more anxious to please the Liberals than to interpret Parnell's views, she took upon herself the task of acting as emissary to Gladstone, and, unknown to O'Shea, she wrote her first letter to Downing Street.

In this letter she wrote of Parnell and of his associates, most of whom she disliked: "It has taken me nearly two years to penetrate his habitual reserve and suspicion of the Saxon mind, and induce him to make his views known at all thereby shaking himself free from the set, by which he was surrounded and who have never had a beneficial effect on their country."

Small wonder that the name of Kitty O'Shea remains anathema in Ireland. Some still believe she was a paid agent of the British government, hired to seduce Parnell! But Mrs. O'Shea had no real interest in Ireland or Irish Home Rule; she was only concerned with her husband's advancement and her lover's prestige.

In view of the ambiguous situation, Gladstone tried to avoid seeing Mrs. O'Shea, but the lady was insistent. She alone was in a position to produce confidential telegrams from Parnell in which he promised to follow her advice. She alone was in a position to offer Gladstone the support of the Irish vote.

Seven years later, Gladstone might say with pious indignation that he had never suspected Parnell of being an adulterer. But in 1883 the Liberal whip was already warning him not to get involved with a woman known to be Parnell's mistress, to which Gladstone, with true Victorian hypocrisy, replied that he refused to believe "that a man could be so dishonourable as to use his mistress as a political agent." At

the moment he said this, he had a letter from her in his pocket, promising Parnell's support in four Ulster constituencies provided the Liberals adopt her husband as candidate for mid-Armagh!

But Liberal support was not enough to procure Captain O'Shea a seat in Parliament, so Kitty nagged Parnell until he committed the first political blunder of his career. He forced the people of Galway to accept O'Shea. In his way, Parnell was as cynical a politician as any, for when the elections of 1884 brought the Tories back into power, he showed himself just as willing to bargain with them as with the Liberals. To be sure, he had no sentimental allegiance to either party, though he still pinned his hopes on Gladstone. In 1885, with the Tories in office, he entrusted Mrs. O'Shea with a secret document that was, in effect, a proposed constitution for Ireland. Gladstone was too cautious a statesman to commit himself, but Home Rule was in the air. By the following winter, it hovered like a cloud over London gatherings, dividing families and closing the gates of the great Whig houses to "the Grand Old Man of English politics," who at seventy-six was preparing to shed the family connections that had hitherto been his main ballast in public life and to tilt a lance for Ireland against the impregnable wall of British prejudice.

On April 8, 1886, Gladstone moved for the first reading of the Home Rule Bill amid scenes of unparalleled excitement. For a short while the majesty of his presence and the magic of his voice subjugated his audience. Men forgot the wranglings of the Cabinet, the defection of the great Whig peers, the pressure of Parnell, and the bitterness of public feeling. But the following morning the ordinary Englishman reading his *Times* interpreted Gladstone's speech in a more prosaic way. To the average taxpayer the Home Rule Bill was a threat to the integrity of the Empire and an abject surrender to the Irish rebels.

With the second reading of the bill, it became clear that some of Gladstone's

ministers would insist on compromises that would restrict it in the end to the measure of self-government already proposed by Chamberlain. For the past week Parnell had been bargaining with Gladstone, fighting for the best terms he could get, remaining throughout as hardfisted as an Irish peasant and showing neither gratitude nor consideration for the old man's courage. He did not believe in British generosity; the English people, he thought, would do only what he, Parnell, could make them do.

On June 7 the debate on the Home Rule Bill came to an end, and that night Parnell, pleading his country's cause in slow, vibrating tones, delivered one of the greatest speeches of his life. Never had he shown such mastery of the situation, never had his words been so humane. But the bill was rejected, 343 to 313. Joseph Chamberlain and his "cabal," helped by the Tories, had succeeded in killing it.

Another election brought the Tories back into power, and with them came the return of coercion and a renewed agrarian rebellion. Outrages and consequent reprisals equaled each other in savagery. At this crucial time Parnell fell seriously ill, leaving his colleagues without direction or a clear-cut policy. He had always been inclined to surround himself with secrecy, and his dislike of being spied upon was well known. But it now led his disappointed followers to picture him as "frivolling with Mrs. O'Shea," when in reality he was near death in a South London nursing home. Weeks of insomnia and nervous attacks had brought him to the verge of madness. In judging Parnell's actions in the last few years of his life, we must remember that he was sick in both mind and body.

At the height of the agrarian troubles in Ireland, the *Times* published certain documents calculated to annihilate Parnell and Parnellism. A black bag left on a Paris railway-station platform was said to have contained papers showing Parnell to be guilty of "incitement to crime and in league with the Phoenix Park murderers." That the editor of the

Times—the leading government journal—should have accepted these documents as authentic showed the lengths to which the Tories were prepared to go to destroy the Irish leader.

On April 18, 1887, the *Times* published a letter, with Parnell's forged signature, in which he apparently "admitted connivance or at least sympathy with the assassins of Lord Frederick Cavendish." To the majority of the English public who regarded the *Times* as sacrosanct, this letter spelled the end of Home Rule and the Liberal party. For Parnell it was the last straw. The *Pall Mall Gazette* had started a campaign of slander, alluding in glaring headlines to the Irish leader's suburban retreat at Eltham and giving salacious details of his liaison with Mrs. O'Shea. Willie could no longer ignore the sneers of his colleagues. His position as a Nationalist member had become untenable, and he was forced to resign. There were stormy scenes at Eltham, and it became clear that only the life of a woman in her nineties prevented Captain O'Shea from coming out into the open to destroy Parnell. At first the Irish leader believed Willie to be responsible for the forged letter, and it prevented him from suing the *Times* for libel.

Parnell's hand was forced when a former member of his party brought an action against the *Times*. Thus began the long-drawn-out drama of the "*Times* Commission case," during which Parnell and the whole of the Irish party stood in the dock, besmirched with every foul accusation their enemies could think of. But after months of despair came victory and full vindication: the forger proved to be a certain Richard Piggott, a discredited journalist

who had hoped to make money out of the Unionist party. The "greatest newspaper in the world" had to pay damages and humbly apologize to the Irish leader.

The dramatic revelations of the court turned the tide of Home Rule. Parnell was now the lion of the day and even the most hidebound Tory squires were willing to shake hands with the man who a few weeks before had been labeled a traitor and an assassin. When Parnell entered the House of Commons on the night of March 1, 1890, he received an ovation rarely accorded even to a Prime Minister. Every hostess in London begged him to honor her parties, and the summer of 1890 saw him as Gladstone's guest at Hawarden, the Prime Minister's country residence. At the very hour of Parnell's triumph, however, the clouds were gathering over Eltham, where Kitty was at the bedside of her dying aunt. She knew that Mrs. Wood's death, while making her financially independent, would enable O'Shea to pose as the injured husband. Parnell foresaw the squalor of the divorce court, but he never imagined that his own people would disown him.

Mrs. Benjamin Wood died at Eltham in the early summer of 1890. In the same week that Parnell was staying at Hawarden with the Prime Minister, Captain and Mrs. O'Shea had a dreadful quarrel, and O'Shea filed for divorce on the grounds of his wife's adultery with Charles Stewart Parnell. There can be no doubt that Mrs. Wood's will played a prominent part in the downfall of the Irish statesman. By leaving her entire fortune to Kitty, she antagonized Willie, who felt cheated of money he thought should be his. It had been bitter

enough for Willie to witness Parnell's triumph, a triumph in which he had no share, but this was the crowning bitterness. He had sacrificed much in pursuit of the Wood inheritance, and now felt he had no alternative but to make common cause with Kitty's brothers and sisters, who were contesting the will. There were also other means of retrieving his finances. Prominent Liberal Unionists, certain that Parnell would be ruined by a divorce, were anxious to know whether Captain O'Shea would be willing to take proceedings. The *Times* people also had an interest in a divorce; it would help them—they thought—to regain the prestige they had lost before the special commission.

After Captain O'Shea filed suit, citing Parnell as corespondent, Parnell and Mrs. O'Shea moved to Brighton, followed by the press. Parnell received the news of the divorce with equanimity—almost with joy—as putting an end to the subterfuge, but Katherine saw it differently. If only Willie had waited a few months, she could have bought him off with the twenty thousand pounds he demanded as the price of his silence. But the will was in probate, and owing to severe financial difficulties of his own, Parnell could not help her. Nor would he do anything to block the divorce, for he now had only one wish—to marry her as soon as possible.

The effect of the divorce was shattering. To the horror of Gladstone and his colleagues, Parnell made no attempt to prepare a defense. Kitty, on the contrary, foolishly brought a counteraction against her husband, naming her sister as corespondent. The public was

STATEMENT OF OWNERSHIP, MANAGEMENT, AND CIRCULATION (Act of August 12, 1970; Section 3685, Title 39, U.S. Code)

1. Title of publication: HORIZON
2. Date of filing: October 1, 1972
3. Frequency of issue: quarterly
4. Location of known office of publication: 1221 Avenue of the Americas, N.Y., N.Y. 10020
5. Location of the headquarters or general business offices of the publishers: 1221 Avenue of the Americas, N.Y., N.Y. 10020
6. Names and addresses of Publisher, Editor, and Managing Editor: Publisher, Paul Gottlieb, 1221 Avenue of the Americas, N.Y., N.Y. 10020; Editor, Charles L. Mee, Jr., 1221 Avenue of the Americas, N.Y., N.Y. 10020; Managing Editor, Shirley Tomkievicz, 1221 Avenue of the Americas, N.Y., N.Y. 10020
7. Owner: American Heritage Publishing Co., Inc., 1221 Avenue of the Americas, N.Y., N.Y. 10020. Names and addresses of stockholders owning or holding 1 per cent or more of total amount of stock of American Heritage Publishing Co., Inc.: McGraw-Hill, Inc., 1221 Avenue of the Americas, N.Y., N.Y. 10020.
8. Known bondholders, mortgagees, and other security holders owning or holding 1 per cent or more of total amount of bonds, mortgages, or other securities: none

9. For optional completion by publishers mailing at the regular rates (Section 132.121, Postal Service Manual). 39 U.S.C. 3626 provides in pertinent part: "No person who would have been entitled to mail matter under former section 4359 of this title shall mail such matter at the rates provided under this subsection unless he files annually with the Postal Service a written request for permission to mail matter at such rates."

In accordance with the provisions of this statute, I hereby request permission to mail the publication named in Item 1 at the reduced postage rates presently authorized by 39 U.S.C. 3626.   Paul Gottlieb, Publisher

10. For completion by nonprofit organizations authorized to mail at special rates: not applicable.
11. Extent and nature of circulation:

	Average No. Copies Each Issue During Preceding 12 Months	Actual No. of Copies of Single Issue Published Nearest to Filing Date
A. Total No. Copies Printed (Net Press Run)	124,400	125,100
B. Paid Circulation		
1. Sales through dealers and carriers, street vendors, and counter sales	1,400	800
2. Mail Subscriptions	115,600	112,100
C. Total Paid Circulation	117,000	112,900
D. Free Distribution (including samples) by Mail, Carrier, or Other Means	3,200	1,400
E. Total Distribution (Sum of C and D)	120,200	114,300
F. Office Use, Leftover, Unaccounted, Spoiled After Printing	4,200	10,800
G. Total (Sum of E and F—should equal net press run shown in A)	124,400	125,100

I certify that the statements made by me above are correct and complete.

Paul Gottlieb, Publisher

thus regaled with all the details of furtive meetings, of houses rented under assumed names, of Parnell's arriving at Eltham in strange disguises. Letters were read that left the public no illusions as to the character of either husband or wife, but it was Parnell who became the target of music-hall jokes and smutty limericks. As expected, the verdict went against him.

At first it seemed as if his powerful personality and almost mythical prestige would triumph over public opinion. For a week there was silence from both the Catholic hierarchy and the Liberal leaders, and the Nationalists rallied enthusiastically to their leader. Gladstone stayed his hand, waiting for the Irish leader to announce his temporary retirement from politics. Finally, however, the old statesman wrote Parnell to say that in view of the scandal he must resign. But this crucial letter never reached Parnell. At Brighton it fell into the hands of an angry, overwrought woman, who tore it up in disgust at the hypocrisy of a man who for ten years had known of the relations between her and Parnell. It was now only a matter of days before the Catholic clergy, led by Cardinal Manning, joined in the condemnation.

On November 25 the Irish members met to re-elect Parnell chairman. There was widespread confusion among the Liberals, for Gladstone's letter had led them to believe that Parnell would not be seeking the position: they were staggered to see him taking the chair as coolly as if there were no stain on his reputation. For the first and last time Parnell spoke in his own defense, giving an accurate version of the divorce proceedings and assuring his hearers that he had never accepted so much as a piece of bread that O'Shea had paid for. But he forgot that most of the men he was speaking to were devoted Catholics, with very little sympathy for worldly values or human weaknesses. In supporting this Protestant adulterer, they acted against their consciences.

They had no sooner come out of the committee room than they were be-

THE O'SHEA-PARNELL DIVORCE CASE.

Full and Complete Proceedings.

PRICE - - - - - 10 CENTS.

BOSTON: NATIONAL PUBLISHING COMPANY, Box 1329.

Parnell's face is on the cover of this pamphlet published in the United States by angry Irish Catholics wishing to discredit him.

sieged by a crowd of outraged Liberals who accused them of having betrayed Gladstone in re-electing Parnell, telling the Irish members of the famous letter, of which the majority knew nothing. That evening Gladstone's letter was published, and with that the Home Rule Bill was set aside for another twenty years. Parnell became once more the fighting guerrilla leader icily indifferent to English opinion, addressing his manifestoes only to the people of Ireland. Bitterest of all was his realization that Gladstone was now his rival for the affections of the Irish people.

Three weeks after the verdict in the divorce court, the struggle for the leadership of the Irish party ended in defeat. Up to the last, Parnell had been confident of victory. He simply could not imagine that two-thirds of his own party would prefer Gladstone to himself. "Surely no Irishman wants an English master," he told them. The words hung in the air, whereupon Tim Healy, a former supporter, snarled in reply, "It's better than an English mistress." At that Parnell lost control, and with a face contracted in fury he turned on Healy as if to strike "the cowardly little scoundrel who dares in an assembly of Irishmen to insult a woman." It was a

tragic breakup of a great party. Of the seventy members present, only twenty-six voted with Parnell.

Two days later the defeated leader crossed over to Dublin. Here the population was still loyal. He was acclaimed by vast crowds as he drove through the streets at the head of a torchlight procession. But though Dublin remained loyal, the "mud cabin" vote was solidly against him.

Six months later he married Kitty O'Shea in a little Sussex registry office on a beautiful June day. In Ireland the marriage rekindled the general bitterness and accentuated the hostility of the priests. Parnell now knew that he could never bring his wife "home to Avondale" and that all his plans for the future would remain hopeless daydreams. His health was deteriorating fast. Crippled with rheumatism, he still went to Ireland every week to speak for his candidates in the upcoming by-elections; but the magic of his presence could no longer spell victory for his nominees. At Kilkenny his opponents even went so far as to flaunt a woman's shift as the banner of Kitty O'Shea.

For a time he felt a certain fierce exultation in the fight, but after a series of humiliating defeats he realized that he could never regain his place in the affections of the Irish people. A young boy of Irish-Spanish extraction called Eamon de Valera was present at one of his last meetings in County Clare. He still remembers the tall, emaciated figure with the straggling beard and the strange, burning eyes standing bareheaded on a rain-swept platform. At one point an old woman came up to him and cried, "May God forgive you, Mr. Parnell, you've broken my heart." She might have left those words unsaid had she known that she was speaking to a dying man. A week later Parnell died at Brighton in the arms of the woman for whose sake he had sacrificed both himself and his country.

Joan Haslip's most recent book is The Crown of Mexico, *a history of Maximilian and Carlota published last year.*

Hemingway:
The Image and the Shadow

He created a dazzling public persona for himself and
mostly lived up to it. He seldom spoke
of how deep his war wounds had gone and what psychic
jackals stalked his later years

By MALCOLM COWLEY

Early and late in life, Hemingway was an extraordinary person. Even the first photographs, after those in baby clothes, reveal the unusual power he had of projecting himself. He looks straight at the camera, he smiles that warm smile of his, and his sisters—as later his companions in fishing or skiing—fade into the background; everyone fades except his big, smiling, square-faced mother, who had something of the same power. Perhaps his lifelong grudge against his mother was based on early rivalry, for Hemingway had a passionate desire to be first in everything. If he couldn't be first in a sport, he abandoned it, as he abandoned football after his senior year at Oak Park High School, where he didn't star on that year's championship team; the prospect of having to play more football was one of the reasons he gave for not going on to college. He had been first, however, in writing for the school paper, and writing was to be the trade he followed for the rest of his life.

There are other early traits to be mentioned. Besides writing stories, he told them to his classmates as if they were ad-ventures of his own. Sometimes they really were, but often they were more vivid and memorable than true. He had a weakness for boasting, usually with the self-deprecatory air that makes boasts more effective. He didn't boast about his studious mind, but, in fact, he applied himself more diligently than his classmates did to any subject that attracted his interest, and he learned almost anything with amazing speed. He was imaginative, enthusiastic, and persistent; also he had more energy than most boys of his age, a talent in itself, and perhaps he already required less sleep than they did.

After being wounded in Italy, he was to spend many sleepless nights. That wound proved to be a decisive event in his career, and he was to make it an event in the lives of a whole generation of writers. It took place on the night of July 8, 1918, a month after he reached the Italian front in a Red Cross ambulance unit and two weeks before his nineteenth birthday. "There was one of those big noises you sometimes hear at the front," Ernest told a friend much later. "I died then. I felt my soul or something coming right out of my body, like you'd pull a silk handkerchief out of a pocket by one corner. It flew around and then came back and went in again and I wasn't dead any more." An ash can, as soldiers called them, fired by an Austrian mortar, had exploded beside him in a forward trench. Badly wounded as he was—later the surgeons counted 237 steel fragments in his legs—Ernest hoisted a still more badly wounded Italian onto his back and plodded off toward the dressing station. On the way he was wounded twice again, by slugs from a heavy machine gun, but somehow he reached the station before he collapsed. It was an exploit that won him the Italian silver cross.

"In the first war I was hurt very badly; in the body, mind, and spirit and also morally," he told me thirty years later. "The true gen is I was hurt bad all the way through and I was truly spooked at the end." Perhaps that was the origin of a contrast between the public and the private Hemingway that was to persist all through his life. Publicly he was a war hero, and a real one, too, considering the courage and instinctive presence of mind he had shown in an emergency. He

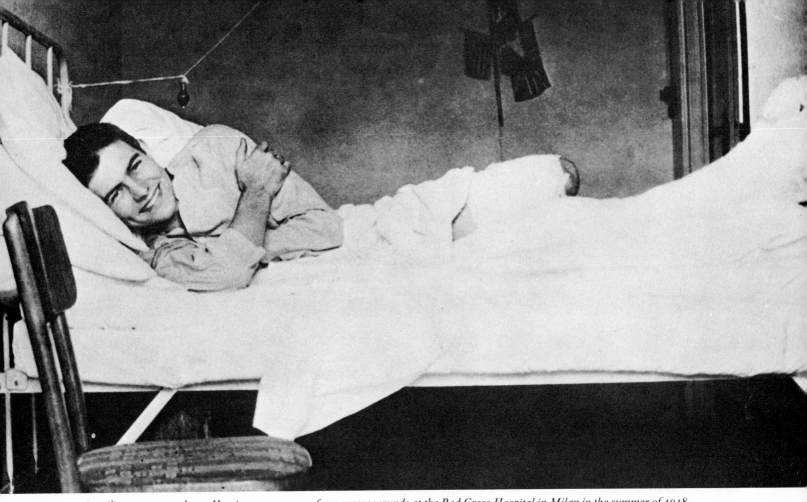

A smiling young war hero, Hemingway recovers from severe wounds at the Red Cross Hospital in Milan in the summer of 1918.

thoroughly enjoyed the role and played up to it like an old trouper. Privately, though, he was, and for a long time would remain, a frightened man. It was not until the Spanish Civil War—or perhaps, so he told me, not until some crazy plane rides over occupied China in the spring of 1941—that he overcame his fear of being blown up at night. Till then he had concealed the fear and challenged himself time and again by deliberately walking into new dangers.

I have a grievance against the enormous and very useful life of Hemingway by Carlos Baker. It tells us what he did and what he said to whom during his long career, but it gives hardly any notion of the immense charm he exerted on his friends, on women, and on older persons he respected. Partly the charm was due to his physical presence: he was tall, handsome, broad-shouldered, with heavy biceps, yet carried himself with a curiously diffident and reassuring air; meeting him was like being led into the box stall of a huge, spirited, but surprisingly gentle stallion. More of the charm depended, though, on his habit of paying undivided attention to each of several persons in turn. He looked in one's eyes, then he turned his head to listen carefully. "Most people never listen," he used to say. Very old men and women, some of them later his enemies, remember with nostalgia his early times in Paris. His first wife, later Mrs. Paul Scott Mowrer, said of him forty years after their divorce, "He was then the kind of man to whom men, women, children, and dogs are attracted. It was something."

About Hemingway's public image a great deal has been written—rhapsodically by journalists and disapprovingly by men of letters, beginning with Edmund Wilson—but it has never been studied with any seriousness. Why shouldn't it be studied? That image has played an important part in fifty years of cultural history. As a matter of fact, it had a history of its own and retained some constant elements while growing through different phases as if it were a person instead of a persona. One phase was that of the young writer living in exile and speaking for the postwar generation with absolute integrity. An-

other was that of the sportsman, traveler, and discriminating drinker, often photographed with a glass in his hand beside the carcasses of enormous fish and mammals. Still other phases were those of the committed man defending the Spanish republic, of the war correspondent ranging through France with a private army, and, in the final years, of the square-faced, grizzly-bearded veteran watching paternally over his flock of young admirers: Mr. Papa.

The image in all its phases, after the first suburban episode of the war hero dazzling his neighbors in Oak Park, played its part on an international stage. Always it was rendered more persuasive by Hemingway's zest for living, by his energy, his passionate desire to be first, and his inborn gift for projecting himself. In one of its phases, that of the sportsman and bon vivant, the image had a discernible effect on a number of commercial enterprises. Years ago, when I was gathering material for a profile, I talked with Jakie Key, a charter-boat captain in Key West. "If you want to say anything bad about Hemingway, don't talk to me," he said.

Hemingway:
For Public
Consumption

Observer in the Spanish Civil War

Big-game hunter in Africa

Dedicated fisherman

"Hemingway made this charter-boat business—he brought the fishermen down." Yes, he brought the fishermen to Key West and Bimini, and bands of hunters to the high African plains, and American college students by the hundreds, then by the thousands, to the festival at Pamplona. Ski resorts in Tyrol and Idaho, bullfights all over Spain, restaurants in Venice, Milan, Paris, Havana—he had good times at all of them, he told with gusto what they had to offer, and the crowds came streaming after.

Of course, the real importance of the Hemingway image has been its effect on literary history. It appeared at exactly the right time: in the early 1920's, when a new generation of American writers was coming forward. Although its members were almost of the same age and strongly shared a feeling of being different from older persons, as late as 1925 they still lacked a collective name, a set of beliefs jointly held, and a code of literary conduct. It should be noted once again that Hemingway gave them the name, after seizing upon a remark of Gertrude Stein's: "You are all a lost generation," she had told him. The younger men accepted the name, which Hemingway himself soon disowned, but they were looking for things that would make them a generation in spirit as well as in biological fact. They especially needed a

sort of older brother on whom they could model themselves as a step for each of them toward achieving a separate identity. Hemingway gave them the older brother, too, in heroes like Nick Adams and Jake Barnes, who quickly became confused with his personal image, and his stories gave them a code of conduct. Like Hemingway, the other new writers would project themselves as being simple, unaffected, tough-spoken, versed in the language of boxing and the bullring, contemptuous of outsiders—especially of those who wrote for money—and brave in an uncomplaining way while suffering from a secret wound.

Here I have to make another distinction of age. The Hemingway image had an effect on some writers of his own age group, notably Fitzgerald and Faulkner (a greater effect in the latter case than has been widely recognized), but Cummings, Wilson, Dos Passos, Hart Crane, and most of the others had already shaped their literary personalities. His strongest immediate influence was on writers, beginning with Steinbeck, who were too young to have served even briefly in the Great War. The influence continued to spread, and it is all-pervasive in the hard-boiled novelists of the 1930's. When still younger novelists wrote about their adventures in the Sec-

ond World War, they produced Hemingway dialogue and Hemingway scenes of action. Often their heroes seemed to be reflections of Robert Jordan among the Spanish guerrillas or of Frederic Henry caught up in the retreat from Caporetto. The Hemingway image was more vivid for them than their own adventures in a different war.

It must be remembered that the image is an essential part of the truth about Hemingway. Not only did he project an idealized picture of himself, but he usually succeeded in living up to it. He had aspirations toward goodness, toward something close to saintliness. When he fell short of his ideal in a fit of professional jealousy or in one of his black rages, he blamed himself and sometimes offered contrite apologies. He was truly a leader of men, foresighted in laying plans for them, incisive in judgment, resourceful and cool-headed in a crisis. He was an outstanding sportsman: an accomplished fisherman, a fair boxer, a good marksman in spite of his impaired vision, and a superb wing shot. He was truly generous to others with his time, and later in life with his money. Beside or beneath these qualities, however, there were others that Hemingway tried to expunge from the picture. They were his shadow side, to borrow a term from Carl Jung, and they included sud-

114

Star reporter in World War II

Amateur boxer

Bullfight aficionado

den rages, hypochondria, fears of death that became a longing for death, and fits of depression that he called "black-assed melancholy." Often he was boastful, truculent, quick to take offense, and he nursed his grudges for a long time. He could no more tolerate rivals—literary rivals in particular—than could an old lion.

After reading *Green Hills of Africa* in 1934, I wrote a little poem—"Ernest," it was called—that I wish had been less prophetic:

Safe is the man with blunderbuss
who stalks the hippopotamus
on Niger's bank, or scours the veldt
to rape the lion of his pelt;

but deep in peril he who sits
at home to rack his lonely wits
and there do battle, grim and blind,
against the jackals of the mind.

But what were the dangers that Ernest faced at home?

According to Jung, "A man cannot get rid of himself in favor of an artificial personality without punishment. Even the attempt to do so brings on, in all ordinary cases, unconscious reactions in the form of bad moods, affects, phobias, compulsive ideas, backslidings, vices, etc." I quote from Jung not because I have any notion of becoming a Jungian critic, but for the special reason that his

formulations cast even more light on Hemingway's problems than do those of Freud. All sorts of Jungian terms seem to apply: not only persona and shadow side, but anima, archetype, and collective unconscious. Moreover, Jung took a special interest in the problems of aging men and women. We read in an article about his theories:

. . . many neuroses, particularly in people during the second half of life, derive from an exaggerated use of one or another function to the exclusion of the others. [Jung named the four functions as thinking, feeling, sensation, and intuition.] An extraverted thinking type, such as a businessman or an engineer, may enter the second half of life having attained all of his rational goals, including financial success and recognition. Nonetheless, these successes and his work no longer bring him the pleasure they once did, and he begins to feel moody and depressed. In such cases, Jung feels that previous goals have lost their capacity to mobilize psychic energy and what the individual needs to do is to realize some other side to his personality, particularly the feeling side.

Such was the diagnosis, with a suggestion for therapy, that Jung seems to have offered to some of the unhappy American tycoons who came to consult him at Bollingen, near Zurich. What would he have said to Hemingway? In those later years Hemingway had attained most of

his rational goals: he was rich, admired, imitated, and almost universally read. Writing well had always been his central ambition, and now he was the most famous writer in the world; the statement would be confirmed by a count of the columns and inches that the press devoted to his exploits and remarks. After the two plane crashes in East Africa, from which he never recovered, he was granted the unique privilege of reading his own obituaries, and these compared in length with the later tributes to Winston Churchill. That same year, 1954, his position was, so to speak, sanctified by the award to him of the Nobel Prize, yet most of the time he was feeling as moody and depressed as the tycoons who made their pilgrimages to Bollingen and begged Jung to help them. Would Jung have offered him the same sort of diagnosis?

In Jung's catalogue of types, Hemingway as a public figure—though not in private—was clearly an extraverted man of sensation. Would Jung have said that he was tired of his persona; that it had ceased to mobilize his psychic energy; that the persona had begun to weaken the subjective force of his writing by substituting itself for his proper heroes (as it did in his long sea novel, *Islands in the Stream*)? Would Jung have advised him to cultivate some repressed side of his personality, for example, the side on which he was clearly an introverted intellectual? One has a brief vision of Hemingway retiring into solitude to write a handbook of fiction or an *Apologia Pro Vita Sua.* It is a fascinating picture, but hardly one for which Hemingway would have been willing to sit as a model.

After the disaster in East Africa, it was too late for simple therapeutic measures. It was even too late for a return to the Catholic Church, a step that Jung might have advised him to take as a means of surmounting his inner problems. Hemingway had lived too hard, and it would seem that he was older physiologically than by the calendar. He had suffered too many internal injuries, he had been battered on the head as often as a punch-drunk fighter, and he no longer had enough resilience to go back to an old faith or adopt a new style of life or undertake a new approach to writing. Besides all that, he was committed to his public image. He was also tired of it, perhaps, but it still had immense rewards to offer him.

What proved to be the greatest of these, and the last that he truly enjoyed, was a triumphal visit to Spain in the summer of 1959. Hemingway toured the country with Antonio Ordóñez, who was competing *mano a mano* with his brother-in-law Luis Miguel Dominguín for recognition as the number-one matador. Antonio was the son of Cayetano Ordóñez, who had been portrayed in *The Sun Also Rises* as the heroic Pedro Romero, and Ernest felt a paternal pride in his exploits. Everywhere he and the younger Ordóñez went, they were cheered by the crowds. At Pamplona, where they spent the week of the *feria,* July 6 to 12, the crowds were bigger than ever and Hemingway was mobbed by younger admirers, including pretty girls. He found time, though, for picnics on the Irati River, where the trout had come back and some of the virgin beech forest was still standing. "Make it all come true again," he had prayed at the end of *Death in the Afternoon.* Most of it came true during that week in Pamplona, with adulatory crowds in the background. "You know," he said to Aaron Hotchner, "it's all better than *The Sun Also Rises.*"

Later, at Málaga, there was his sixtieth birthday party, which lasted for twenty-four hours, with champagne from Paris, Chinese foods from London, fireworks from Valencia, and a shooting booth from a traveling carnival. Ordóñez and the Maharajah of Cooch Behar stood meekly in the booth while Ernest shot cigarettes from between their lips; then Ernest organized the guests into a *riau-riau* that snaked through the shrubbery. A rocket lodged in the top of a royal palm and blazed there until the fire department arrived in a truck that it must have borrowed from a Mack Sennett comedy. The guests stayed for breakfast. It might have been all the grand parties of the 1920's packed into one, and it was Ernest's valedictory. Afterward everything turned bitter. The competition between the two great matadors ended when Dominguín was badly gored. Ordóñez spent a month in jail for using picadors who had been suspended. Hemingway went back to Idaho and then to Havana to write a story of the trip for *Life* magazine. The story got out of control and became a rambling, boastful manuscript nearly three times as long as the forty thousand words that *Life* had agreed to print. Hemingway kept struggling with it, but found himself unable to cut it down to size or bring it up to his own standards. Finally the revisions had to be made by Hotchner and the magazine editors.

During the year that followed his last grand summer, Hemingway's body was visibly dwindling away and his mind suffered even more. One might apply Jung's words to him and say that the traits of character he concealed from the world and repressed into his unconscious were rising again to haunt him in outlandish forms. Always suspicious of people's motives, he now began to dream of a vast conspiracy against him in which most of his friends had involved themselves after selling out to the FBI. He would leave a restaurant in the middle of dinner if he saw two strangers drinking together. "Those two FBI men at the bar," he would say in a low voice after looking hard at two traveling salesmen. "Don't you think I know an FBI man when I see one?" He had other fears, of dying in penury or of being clapped into jail for mild infractions of the game laws. His lifelong aggressiveness and his killer instinct were being turned against himself, the last of his possible trophies.

Still, after relinquishing the manuscript of *The Dangerous Summer,* he went back to his writing table every morning in the effort to finish another book that might, in this case, be truer than life. He regarded writing as a trade that was never to be mastered, and he said more than once, "I'm apprenticed out at it until I die." In the spring before his death he was planning to revise *A Moveable Feast,* but found that he had been too deeply wounded to write even a single line. "I can't finish the book. I *can't,*" he confided over the telephone to Hotchner. "I've been at this goddamn worktable all day, standing here all day, all I've got to get is this one thing, maybe only a sentence, maybe more, I don't know, and I can't get it. Not any of it. You understand, I *can't.*" That confession of failure came almost at the end; for every practical purpose it *was* the end. In one respect and only one, Hemingway resembled Hart Crane, who was born on the same day and whom he outlasted by nearly thirty years: both of them felt that if they couldn't write, they didn't want to live.

Malcolm Cowley, who lived among Hemingway's "lost generation" in Paris in the 1920's, published Exile's Return *in 1934. He has since been a leading critic, editor, and historian of letters at home.*

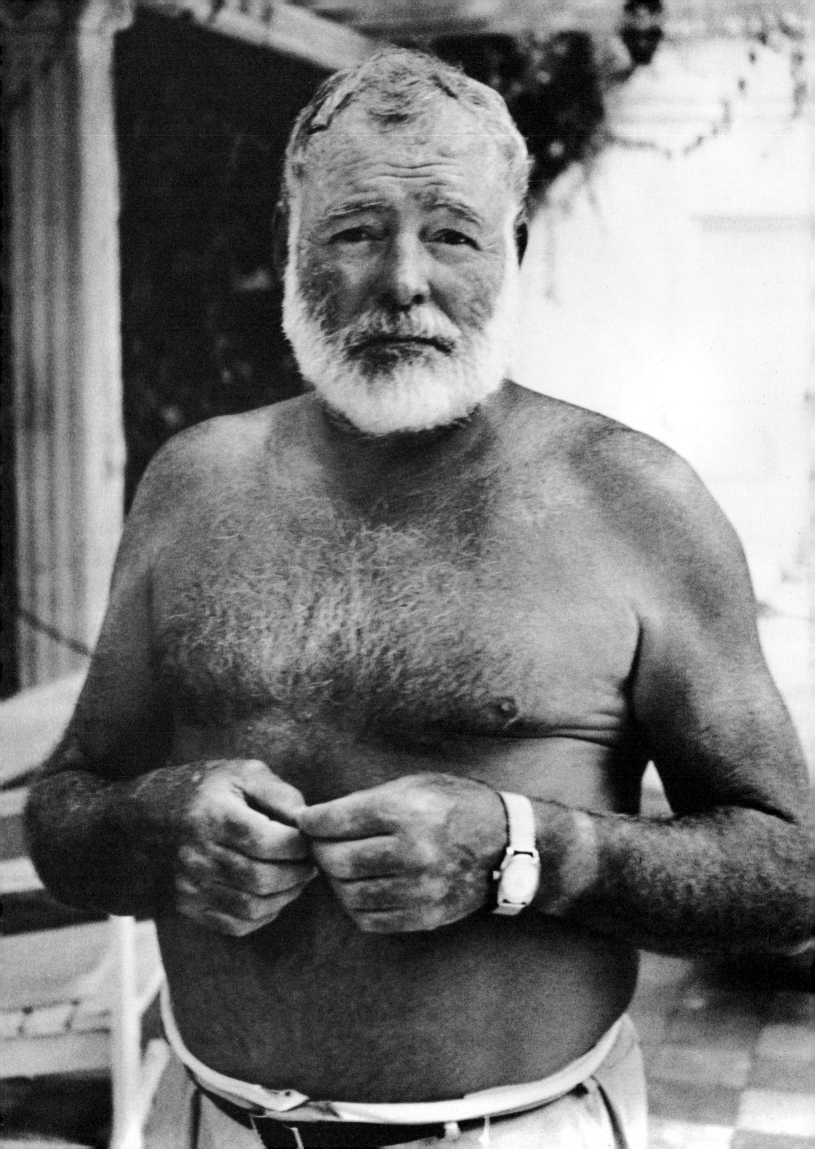

Continental Drip

Geophysicists of the world, are you ready? Here, hard on the heels of drift,
comes another earth-shaking new theory derived from simply looking at maps

By ORMONDE DE KAY, JR.,
FELLOW OF THE ROYAL GEOGRAPHICAL SOCIETY*

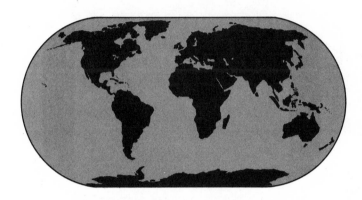

In 1620 Francis Bacon, perusing maps of the New World, noticed that its east coast would, if tilted, fit snugly up against the Old World's west coast. He concluded that the Americas had once been joined to Europe and Africa. Almost three centuries later, in 1903, a young German meteorology student named Alfred Wegener reached the same conclusion from the same data, and in 1911 he began to piece together the hypothesis that came to be called the theory of continental drift.

Drift theory, as elaborated by Wegener's successors after his death in 1930, held that all of the world's far-flung land surfaces had originally coexisted in a single supercontinent, Pangaea ("all lands"). Some two hundred million years ago Pangaea broke up into two lesser supercontinents, Laurasia in the north and Gondwanaland in the south. The former eventually divided into North America, Greenland, and Eurasia (except India), and the latter into South America, Africa, Antarctica, Australia, and India.

This notion of the earth's land crust as a gigantic jigsaw puzzle perpetually unsolving itself was an instant hit with magazine editors—the public loved it —but most scientists dismissed it as childish nonsense. Then, in the 1950's and 1960's, came the first concerted international effort to study the earth as a whole. It was found that the ocean floors are traversed by mountain ranges thousands of miles long. These oceanic ridges are zones of frequent earthquakes: periodically magma

spews forth from fissures in them to spill down their slopes and widen the seabeds on either side.

Here at last was a force powerful enough to displace continents. Scientists perceived that the lines of seismic activity along the oceanic ridges—and along the great circumpacific earthquake belt as well as along certain earthquake belts extending overland —mark, in effect, the boundaries of immense "plates" on which the continents "drift." Wegener's crazy notion suddenly became respectable. Its last opponents capitulated, and today the once-despised theory of continental drift is accepted everywhere as fact.

Both Bacon and Wegener, we now know, read their maps aright.

Well, I, too, have been looking at maps, and I, too, have been struck by a revelation no less global in scope. From it I have constructed a hypothesis, which I call, provisionally, the theory of continental drip.

As the term suggests, continental drip is the tendency of land masses to drip, droop, sag, depend, or hang down—like the wet paint in the Sherwin-Williams trademark, except that they cling to the earth's surface below

the equator instead of falling off into space. The cartographic evidence for drip is at least as impressive as that for drift. It is, indeed, as plain as the nose on your face—and probably more pendulous.

Let's look at the world map. Africa and South America— those very land masses, by coincidence, whose congruent coasts first inspired both Bacon and Wegener to their wild surmise—are textbook examples of drip, with their broad tops and tapering lower extremities. But so is North America, with Baja California and Florida dangling down at its sides. Greenland, too, clearly shows the characteristics of drip.

Of Europe's major projections, all except Jutland hang down, but with a difference: Scandinavia and Iberia droop south*west*, while Italy and Greece droop south*east*. These departures from the vertical are caused by continental drift: Eurasia is drifting eastward, dragging the first two peninsulas behind it. As for the second two, they are paralleled by two earthquake zones—"plate boundaries"—that extend, respectively, between the Alps and the Aegean and between the eastern end of the Black Sea and the northwestern corner of Iran. The Crimea, incidentally, is another example of continental drip.

In Asia we find a consistent record of drippage. From its southern flank droop pendulous India, then the spindly Malay Peninsula, and finally, sagging Indochina (Southeast Asia). Ascending the continent's east coast, we encounter the small Luichow Penin-

*In arrears

sula (with the island of Hainan just below it), Korea, and Kamchatka. Sakhalin, separated from Siberia near its northern tip by a narrow strait, looks as if it, too, was once a dependent peninsula.

This brings us to the last continent but one, Australia. Australia appears to defy the laws of continental drip—unless, of course, it is the exception that proves the rule. (This strange land mass, we may recall, once seemed to defy the laws of zoology and botany as well.) But since Australia was the last continent to assert its independent identity, still having been attached to Antarctica a mere forty million years ago, it may simply not have been around long enough to show the more pronounced effects of drip. Even so, it does conform in at least one particular to drip theory—as we shall shortly see.

How do islands fit into the picture? To assess their role with respect to continental drip, we must exclude the numerous smaller land masses that lie athwart earthquake zones, and whose situation, orientation, and conformation are therefore affected only intermittently, if at all, by drip. These include, *inter alia*, the Aleutians, Japan, the Philippines, Indonesia, New Guinea, and New Zealand, as well as the West Indies, Iceland, and the islands of the eastern Mediterranean.

By the assumptions of drip theory we would expect earthquake-free islands to extend, as a rule, north-south, and to lie south of large land masses from which they may have dripped. Again the map bears out our expectations: we find Madagascar below the Horn of Africa, Ceylon below India, Tasmania below Australia, Borneo below Southeast Asia, and Hainan, as mentioned, below the bulge of China. (That Madagascar drifted rather than dripped to its present site signifies less than that its orientation and shape clearly reveal the effects of drip.) In the Atlantic, Newfoundland has obviously dripped down from Labrador, and in the relatively earthquake-free Mediterranean, Corsica and Sardinia are

models of drip theory as it applies to islands.

The British Isles were once, as we know, linked by broad land bridges to each other and to Europe. Here again, however, their origin would seem less important than their north-south orientation, caused by drip.

Turning, finally, to the polar regions, we find that the Arctic is an ocean surrounded by land and the Antarctic a land mass surrounded by ocean.

The shorelines ringing the Arctic Ocean are broken and irregular, but no arm of land projects markedly north, and even the few peninsulas extend, in the main, east-west. Of the islands, only Novaya Zemlya shows a pronounced north-south orientation. In general, then, the north coasts of North America, Greenland, and Eurasia are —like those of Africa and South America—long, continuous, and comparatively even in terms of latitude. As such, they present a dramatic contrast to the south coasts of the same land masses, which consist of one or more great tongues of land, hanging down like huge stalactites.

Antarctica's chief significance with respect to drip theory is simply that it is where it is, as far south as it can be. Its conspicuous outflung arm, Antarctic (or Palmer) Peninsula, does not, as might appear, contradict drip theory by "dripping" north; it is simply a small portion of the continent left trailing northward in the wake of Antarctica's southward drift (and, possibly, drip).

If anyone still questions the reality of continental drip, let him turn the world map upside down. The land masses now shoot upward in a giddy profusion of spikes, spires, spindles, knobs, and domes, while the earthquake-free islands rise like captive balloons from their vertiginous "skyline." This global show of energetic upward movement confirms the impression of languid downward drip received earlier—forcefully enough, I should think, to convince the most stubborn skeptic.

How will continental drip affect our world in future ages? Will the land masses gradually slip south to come together again below the equator in New Pangaea? Not at all; such an assumption overlooks the mighty force of drift, which continues to move some land masses *north*. Drift carried India northward four thousand miles, and rammed it up against Eurasia with sufficient impact to raise up the Himalayas—and also, perhaps, to jar Ceylon loose.

Drift and drip are complementary; while the first determines the position of land masses, the second helps determine their shape. Since Pangaea broke up, the continents have presented an ever more drippy appearance. Wherever they may yet wander, then, we can expect some (e.g., Africa) to become more attenuated, and others (e.g., Australia) to be festooned on their undersides, like Asia, with ever more elongated streamers of land.

A vexing question remains: what causes continental drip? A few possible explanations come to mind: some paleomagnetic force, for example, unsuspected and therefore undetected, centered in massive, mountainous Antarctica and perpetually tugging at the lower hems of land masses. Or drip might somehow be the result of the earth's rotation, or of lunar attraction. One conclusion, however, would seem inescapable: contrary to the teachings of science, but as every schoolchild has always known, north really is up, and south down!

Close study of Mars and other planets may show that continental drip is not limited to our own planet. Until then, all that can be predicted with certainty is that the confirmation of drip theory through the identification of its cause will keep armies of scientists busy for years, at vast expense to governments. In the meantime, like Francis Bacon, or, better, like the astronomer Percival Lowell, who posited the existence of Pluto long before that planet was sighted, I am content to have made my own modest contribution by pointing out the way.

A FOUR-FOOTED FOOTNOTE ON BIGNESS

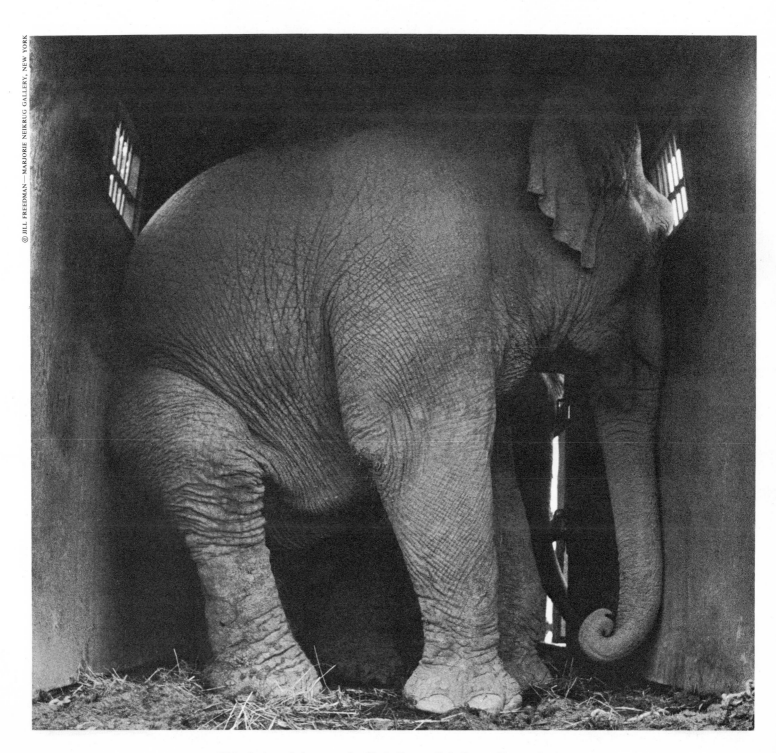

This elephant belongs to the Clyde Beatty-Cole Bros. Circus, the largest traveling tent circus in the world. Periodically, he has to wedge his giant frame into this van and move on to the next performance.

Seventeenth-century Englishmen often kept death's-heads in their houses, or even wore them as ornaments, to remind themselves that life is short. Jill Freedman's photograph of a cramped behemoth might serve as a *memento mori* for our own day: a reminder that "in great size there may be melancholy imperfections."